Fun Devotions for Boys

GOTTA HAVE GOD

Ages 6-9

LEGACY PRESS
www.LegacyPressKids.com

Fun Devotions for Boys

GOTTA HAVE GOD

Ages 6-9

Diane Cory

To my boys, Brian, Brad, and Brett.
To my husband Scott for supporting me during the writing of this book.
To my special friend, Mindy Peterson, for the many hours she spent proofreading and encouraging me and for her constant love and support.

GOTTA HAVE GOD FOR AGES 6-9
©2012 by Legacy Press, twenty-ninth printing
ISBN 10: 1-885358-97-0
ISBN 13: 978-1-885358-97-4
Legacy reorder #LP46962
JUVENILE NONFICTION / Religion / Devotion & Prayer

Legacy Press
P.O. Box 261129
San Diego, CA 92196
www.LegacyPressKids.com

MIX
Paper from
responsible sources
FSC™ C013572

Interior Illustrator: Aline L. Heiser
Cover Illustrator: Helen Harrison

Unless otherwise noted, Scriptures are from the *Holy Bible: New International Version* (North American Edition), copyright ©1973, 1978, 1984 by the International Bible Society. Used by permission of Zondervan Bible Publishers.

Printed in South Korea

TABLE OF CONTENTS

TABLE OF CONTENTS

TABLE OF CONTENTS

INTRODUCTION

Hey, guys, did you know that God wants to be your best buddy? And this book can help you learn more about Him! Use Gotta Have God to get to know your heavenly Father better. As you read each devotion you will find out more about God and how to be a Christian. After you read, there is a cool activity each day to help you understand the Bible.

Here are steps to use Gotta Have God:

1. Read the devotion name and purpose.

2. Read the Bible verse. Look it up in your Bible. Draw a line under the words in your Bible to help you find the verse later. God doesn't mind if you draw a neat line in His Word.

3. Read the story or have your parents read it to you. Answer the questions.

4. Think about the answers to the questions. Pray to God. Talk to God about what you have learned. Try to spend a minute or more just listening for God's voice in your heart and mind.

5. Read the activity directions and do the activity. The projects and puzzles will help you act on what you have learned.

Use this each day in a special time alone with God.

Take time to talk to God in prayer as you go through this book. Start today and learn why you *Gotta Have God!*

GOTTA KNOW GOD

GOD'S AWESOME WORD

The Bible is God's true Word to me.
Every word of God is flawless.

Proverbs 30:5

The Bible Is True

A lie is when someone says something that isn't true. Books that are called "fiction" tell something that isn't true. Fiction stories are made-up stories and they aren't the truth. They may tell part of the truth, but not all the truth. Books are special because they tell us many things. They tell us about trees, animals, clouds and people.

There is one book that tells us the truth. This book stands alone as being the best book of all — the Bible. The word Bible means "The Book." The Bible is God's special book. His Words are written in His Book.

The Bible tells us many things about God and everything He made. It tells us that God made land, sky, stars, sun, moon, animals and people. The Bible tells about God's power and how much He loves us. It tells us God made us.

God told special people what to say and what to write down on each page. Everything in the Bible is true because it comes from God Himself. God never lies!

Your Turn

1. Can you name some things in the Bible that God made?
2. Do you read your Bible each day? Maybe your mom or dad can read the Bible with you. When will you read your Bible each day?

_____

_____

_____

_____

_____

_____

Prayer

Thank You for the Bible and Your words to us. Help me to remember to read the Bible each day. Amen.

SOMETHING WRONG!

Some things aren't true, but the Bible is true. Look at the books below. Circle the one that will help you live the best. Cross out those you should not read. Draw a square around those you might be able to read with caution. The answers are on page 229.

GOD'S AWESOME WORD

The Bible is God's Word.
The word became flesh [a man] *and lived among us.*

John 1:14

Jesus, God's Living Word

The Book. God's Word. The B-I-B-L-E. The Word. The Bible. We call the Bible by many different names.

"Jesus loves me this I know, for the Bible tells me so. " We sing about the Bible.

The Bible is the only book that tells the truth about God. God sent Jesus to be like a living Bible. Jesus is God's Son. He came to tell about Himself and His Father, God. He was like a walking story book, sent to tell about God.

When you look at what Jesus did on earth in the Bible, you see what God is like.

John 5:39 says, "The Scriptures testify [tell] about me." Do you want to know what God is like? Read God's stories in the Bible and you will know God.

Your Turn

1. Why is the Bible a good book for you to read?
2. How does learning about Jesus help you learn about God?

_____

_____

_____

_____

_____

_____

Prayer

Thank You, God, for Jesus, the living Word of God. Help me to read my Bible each day so I can know what God is like. Help me to learn about Jesus so I can know God. Amen.

JESUS SAID

Can you decode the Jesus' words in the Bible below? The answer is on page 229.

A B C D E F G H I J K L M N
1 2 3 4 5 6 7 8 9 10 11 12 13 14

O P Q R S T U V W X Y Z
15 16 17 18 19 20 21 22 23 24 25 26

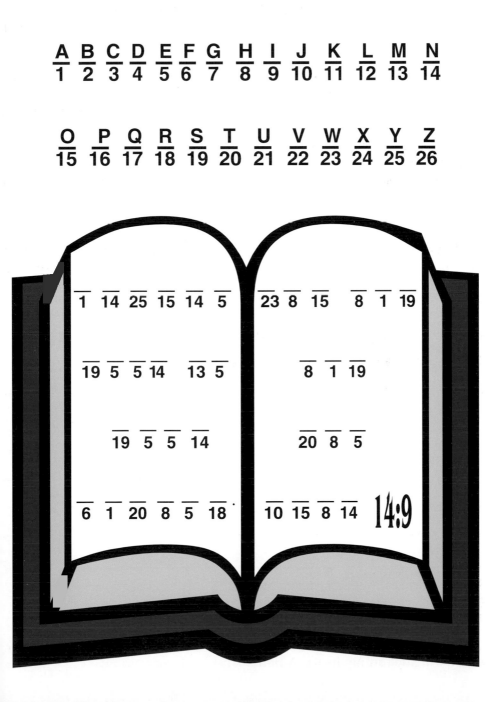

1 14 25 15 14 5   23 8 15   8 1 19

19 5 5 14   13 5   8 1 19

19 5 5 14   20 8 5

6 1 20 8 5 18 .   10 15 8 14   14:9

GOD'S AWESOME WORD

Bible words stick with me.
How sweet are your words to my taste, sweeter
than honey to my mouth.

Psalm 119:103

Peanut Butter

"Someone is at the door!" yelled Mom.

"I'll get it," said Kenny as he ran to the door.

"Hello," a small voice called. "Would you like to buy some peanut butter cookies to help our scout troop?"

"Mom," called Kenny, "this boy is selling peanut butter cookies. Can we get a box? Please! I love peanut butter. It tastes sweet and sticks to the roof of my mouth. Besides, I want to help out the scout troop."

"Sure," said Mom. "A peanut butter and jelly sandwich sounds good for lunch. For dessert we can eat a peanut butter cookie."

God's Word, the Bible is like peanut butter in some ways. God's words are sweet like peanut butter. When God tells of His love for the world it is sweet and it sticks. People remember these sweet words.

Bible verses should stick (stay) in your heart when you read them. Then you will want to read the Bible more because it is good and it sticks with you. You will remember God's Word to help you obey your parents and teachers.

Tell others about the sweetness of God's Word so they can know Jesus, too.

Your Turn

1. How is God's Word like peanut butter?
2. What does it mean when something sticks? How can the Bible stick?
3. Do you know a Bible verse or story that is sweet to you?

_____

_____

_____

_____

Prayer

Thank You, God, for Your sweet verses that tell us You love us. I pray Your words will stick in my heart. Amen.

THE PEANUT BUTTER JAR

Look at the jar of peanut butter. Fill it with words from the Bible that will stick in your mind. You can write favorite verses from this book in the jar. Fill it each day with a new or old verse as you learn God's words.

GOD'S AWESOME WORD

God wants to talk to you and me.
All Scripture is God breathed.
2 Timothy 3:16

God Talks To Me

Mom whispered in Josh's ear, "You're a great kid."

Josh whispered back in her ear, "You're a great mom."

Someone in your family talks to you every day. Grandparents and friends talk to you on the telephone. Maybe you talk to the mailman or the crossing guard at school.

God wants to talk to you each day. He gave the Bible as one way to talk to you. He gave the Bible so He can talk to you about His care. He gave you the Bible so He can talk to you about His creation. He gave you the Bible so He can talk to you about His love.

God does want to talk to you! He wants to talk to you about how you live your life. The Word of God was written many years ago, but it is good for you today.

Reading the Bible is like hearing God talk. All the Bible says is from God. Just like a letter from a friend tells you what that person is doing, God's words tell you what He has done and will do. God's Word is a special letter written to you because God loves you.

Your Turn

1. God can talk to you when we read the Bible. How can you talk to Him?

2. The word of God is active! What does that mean?

_____

_____

_____

_____

_____

Prayer

God, I want to know You and hear from You. I will believe Your words in the Bible and listen to You. Amen.

BOOK TALK

The Bible is like God's talking book. Pretend you are talking to God by writing a page in your own book to Him. Pretend the page below is from your own book.

GOD'S AWESOME WORD

God wants us to know Him.
Some trust in chariots and horses,
but we trust in the name of the Lord.

Psalm 20:7

Clues About God

"Dad! This is my friend Mark. Mark, this is my dad," Cody said as he introduced the two. "Mark is the new boy in my class at school. He moved here from another town."

"Hi, Mr. Burns!" said Mark. "I'm glad to meet you."

"Nice to meet you too, Mark," said Dad. "Where do you live?"

"In the blue house, next to the fire station on Jones Street."

"Oh! How do you like it here, Mark?" asked Mr. Burns.

"So far, I like it!" said Mark.

When you meet someone it is good to know his or her name. Names are like clues that help tell us who people are.

God gives us clues about Himself in the Bible. Isaiah 42:8 says, "I am the Lord, that is my name." God wants you to know Him as well as you know your family. That is why He gives you clues to know Him. He already knows everything about you. Matthew 10:30 says, "Even the hairs on your head are numbered."

Your Turn

1. How can you explain to others who you are?
2. How does God give us clues about Himself?
3. How can you give others clues about God?

_____

_____

_____

_____

_____

Prayer

Thank You, God, that I can meet new people. Teach me to give others clues about You. Amen.

MAGNIFYING GLASS

Write the names of friends and family on the magnifying glass below. Give clues for each person that would tell others about them. Pray for each person each day.

GOD'S AWESOME NAMES

God gave me a special name.
Our help is in the name of the Lord.

Psalm 124:8

Tell Me Something

Alex Alex Alex.

Mitch Mitch Mitch.

What if people had the same first, middle and last names? People wouldn't seem very special. Names help tell about someone or something. The fast food name "Burger Giants" tells that the hamburgers there are big. The person who named you had a reason for giving you your name.

Some people in the Old Testament of the Bible were called Hebrews. The Hebrews were God's first people. Each Hebrew boy had a name that told something about him. The boy's name was the greatest thing hoped for in that child. For example, Samuel means "the name of God" His parents wanted him to tell others about God.

Noah means "comforter." Noah's parents hoped he would comfort people who were sad. Moses means "taken from the water" because he was put in a basket in the river to protect him from the king. The princess took him from the water to care for him.

A name tells us what people are like and who they are. God gave you a special name!

Your Turn

1. How did your parents choose your name? Look up the story of your name in a book of names. Ask your parents how you got your name.
2. What is your middle name? Ask a friend what his or hers is.
3. Why do you think God wants you to know His name?

_____

_____

_____

_____

Prayer

Thank You, God, for my name. Teach me more about Your name, God. I want to know You. I want to tell others about You. Amen.

MY STORE

The sign in front of a store tells the name of the store and something about the store. Write your own store name in the front of the store and put your name on the store window. Remember that God loves your name.

GOD'S AWESOME CREATION

God created the heavens and earth.
It is I who made the earth and created mankind upon it.
Isaiah 45:12

God's Tools

Saw, hammer…what tools go into a tool belt?

You can build with a hammer, saw, nails and wood. Imagine creating a tree house without a hammer, wood or nails!

What tools did God use to create the world? He didn't use tools. God only needed to use His powerful voice. He spoke and the heavens and earth appeared in space.

Some of the first words in the Bible say, "God created the heavens and the earth." These words tell us He is a creator. God's tool belt is full of power and might to create what He wants.

Your Turn

1. What do creators do?
2. Why do you think God created the earth?
3. What can you make from tools you have?

_____

_____

_____

_____

_____

_____

_____

Prayer

Thank You, God, for creating the world. Thank You for loving me enough to provide a place for me to live. Amen.

GOD'S TOOL BELT

If God can make the earth, what else can He do? Write what God can do on the tool belt below.

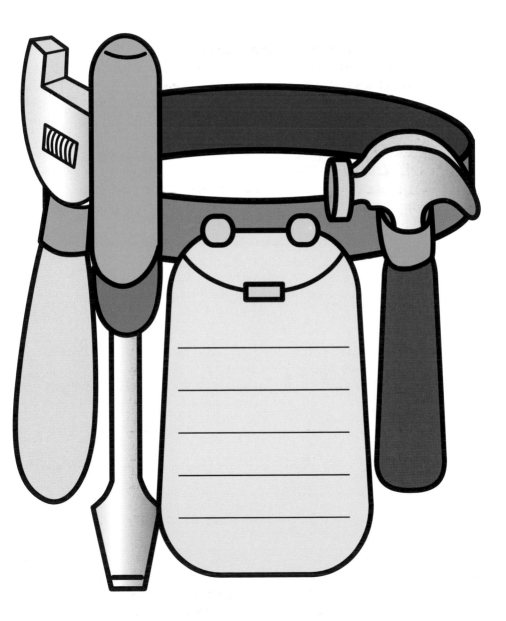

GOD'S AWESOME CREATION

I'm different, because God made me.
God created man in his own image...
male and female he created them.

Genesis 1:27

I'm Not Like Others

Did you know there are no two snow flakes exactly alike?

Did you know that each of your fingers can print a special design? Each person's finger prints are different from anyone else's. The special police force called the FBI studies finger prints to find people who break the law.

There is no one on this earth just like you. God created people to be like Him in special ways. God can smell! Do you have a nose? God can speak! Do you have a mouth? God can see! Do you have eyes? God can hear! Do you have ears?

We don't know what God looks like. God doesn't need to have a body to have a nose, mouth, eyes or ears. God made your body to do what He does without a body.

God is the one who made you different. In Genesis 1:26-28, you can read about how God created people in His image.

Your Turn

1. Why did God create you?
2. Whom do you look like in your family?
3. How are you like God? Can you see how you are made in the image of God?

_____

_____

_____

_____

_____

_____

Prayer

Thank You, God, for my life and for creating me. Amen.

FAMILY FINGERS

Make a finger print of each person in your family on the shapes below (use an ink pad or a dab of paint). Label each print with the family member's name. Use a magnifying glass to see how God made each print different.

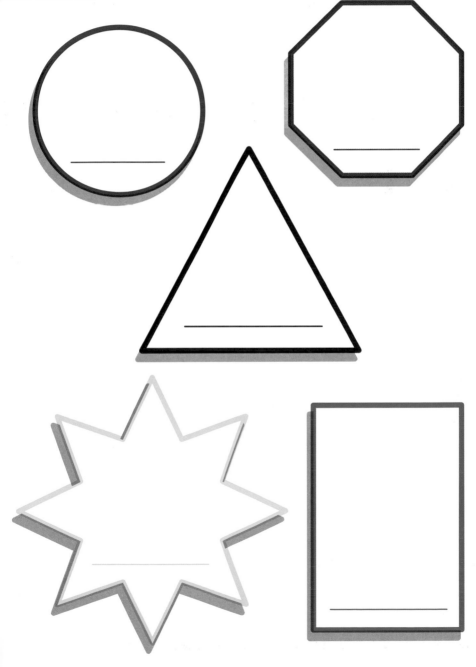

GOD'S AWESOME CREATION

God made all the animals on the earth.
He did not create [the earth] to be empty,
but formed it to be inhabited [filled].

Isaiah 45:18

God's Big Farm

A red barn, shiny tractor, duck pond and many different kinds of animals — what do we call this place? It's a farm!

Have you ever visited a farm? A farm can be a noisy and busy place. Dogs bark, ducks quack, pigs oink, horses neigh and cows moo.

The farmer spends a lot of time feeding and caring for all the animals on his farm. Horses need to be washed, brushed and shoed. Cows need their oats and chicken eggs need to be collected from the hens' nests.

When God created the world, He prepared it for all animals. It is like He created a giant farm. On God's farm there are many, many kinds of animals. There are different shapes and sizes of fish in the ocean. There are different kinds of birds that fly in the sky.

The Bible tells that some animals were tame and some were wild. God created animals that crawl on the ground. He used His power to create the smallest ladybug and the largest dinosaur. He lovingly spoke a blessing for each animal. God even talked to the animals. He told them to grow in their numbers. Read about God creating the animals in Genesis 1:20-25.

Your Turn

1. Why did God make animals?
2. Can you name some animals from the Bible?

_____

_____

_____

_____

_____

Prayer

Thank You, God, for making the animals. I am glad the earth is like a giant farm. Amen.

GOD'S FARM YARD

What is your favorite animal? Draw a picture of it below. What does your animal eat? Draw that, too!

GOD'S AWESOME CREATION

God created the moon — a special flashlight!
He...calls them each by name.

Psalm 147:4

The Day and Night Skies

Could you be an astronaut? Imagine you are the first boy to go to the moon. You would see many stars as your rocket moves toward space.

On a clear night you can see many stars in the sky. They look like they are hanging in space. You could never count the stars in space. Yet God put each one there and gave it a name.

Do you know the name of the star God created for earth? It is the sun! The sun gives light in the day. God wanted you to have light to do your work and play.

The moon was created by God so you can rest at night. The moon and stars make the night sky look like God is shining a flashlight on the earth. Find out more about it in Genesis 1:14-19.

Your Turn

1. Why did God give light?
2. Why do you think God made the stars?
3. Can you find star stories in the Bible? (Hint: Star of Bethlehem)

Prayer

God, I see Your work in the day and night sky. Thank You for being my God and making the night and day skies. Amen.

A FLASHLIGHT AT NIGHT

The moon and stars make the night sky look like God is shining a flashlight on the earth. Can you draw stars and a moon below this flashlight?

GOD'S AWESOME CREATION

God made plants for me to enjoy.
He makes grass grow for the cattle, and plants for man.
Psalm 104:14

Things That Grow

Are you a tree climber? Have you ever played a spy game in the bushes? Without a tree there would be nothing to climb. Without the bushes there would be no spy game.

Did you know God created all the trees and all the bushes? God spoke and the trees appeared. God spoke again and the bushes appeared. He spoke again and the flowers and grass grew.

God wants you to enjoy climbing trees and playing spy. He wants you to enjoy eating apples and other fruit. God can create anything at anytime. He created all the plants for you to enjoy. Read about how God made the plants in Genesis 1:11-13.

Your Turn

1. Which of God's plants do you enjoy?
2. What kinds of fruit and vegetables do you like to eat?

_____

_____

_____

_____

_____

_____

Prayer

I enjoy playing outside where I can see the plants You created, God. Thank You for all Your creations. Amen.

TREE HOUSE CREATION

God made plants for us to enjoy. To remind you of God's plant creations, draw your own tree house in the tree.

GOD'S AWESOME CARE

I'm heard by God.
*You will seek me and find me when you seek me
with all of your heart.*

Jeremiah 29:13

Finding God

"It couldn't have just walked away!"

"I know I put it right here!"

"I'm not stopping until I find it."

Seeking after God is not like looking for a missing pen or a football. When you look for God you can always find Him.

You can't always find other things you look for. God isn't a thing, He is real. Can you talk with your pen or football? Can you call to your pen or ball?

A lost ball may not be found for months. God isn't lost for a day or a week. God has promised to be there when you look for Him. The Bible says in Jeremiah that when you call out to God with your heart, He will come. Call out to Him and He will hear you.

Your Turn

1. Is God real? How do you know He is real?
2. How can you look for God?
3. How can you help others look for God?

_____

_____

_____

_____

_____

_____

Prayer

Thank You, God, that I can call to You and You answer me. I want to seek You with all my heart. Please show me You are there, Lord. Amen.

CALLING GOD

Draw a picture of your face and hair on this figure. Write something you might say to God inside the story bubble.

GOD'S AWESOME CARE

God watches over me.
The Lord will watch over your coming and going.

Psalm 121:8

Firemen & Policemen

Bradley couldn't sleep no matter how hard he tried. He laid in bed tossing and turning. He laid on his side, his back and his stomach. Then he turned to his other side again.

As Bradley counted the sparkles in the ceiling above, he could hear sirens. "Are those sirens police cars or fire trucks?" he wondered.

In his mind Bradley imagined he was a fireman. He pictured himself riding on the back of a big, red fire truck. Protecting the city from fires sounded exciting to him.

His mind wandered back to the sounds. "I'm glad the fireman and policeman are there to protect and defend me," he thought. Then he yawned. Firemen are always at their stations waiting to be called to a fire. You may not be able to see all of the fire trucks or police cars, but they are there anyway to watch over you.

That is the way God is. He is always there watching over you. You may be asleep, but God is there. No matter what time it is, God is there. No matter where you go, God is there.

Your Turn

1. How does God watch over you?
2. How does it make you feel knowing God is watching over you?
3. God will never stop watching over you. How can you show Him that you like His watchful care?

Prayer

Thank You, God, for being there. I am so glad You love me and are there to watch over my days and nights. Amen.

POLICE LIGHTS & FIRE BELLS

God uses people like policemen and firemen and your parents to help watch over you. Write the names of people whom God gives to watch over you on the police light and fire bell.

GOD'S AWESOME CARE

I'm one of God's sheep.
The Lord is my shepherd, I shall not be in want.

Psalm 23:1

My Shepherd

"Go to sleep, Jared," said Mother. "It's time to turn the lights out."

"I can't go to sleep!" Jared replied. "I'm worried about the track and field contest at school tomorrow. I never do well at the 100 yard dash or anything else."

"I'd feel nervous, too, Jared," said Mother. "But, don't worry. Just do the best you can. Besides, God the shepherd will be on the field with you."

"Shepherd? I thought shepherds took care of sheep."

"That's right, Jared." Mother rubbed his neck. "God is like a shepherd and we are like His sheep. He loves you! God wants to help you in all you do. When God helps you, you are like a little lamb to Him.

"Tell me more!" Jared yawned. "I want God to be my shepherd."

Mother saw that he was getting sleepy. "We'll talk about shepherds and sheep more tomorrow night. You need to get to sleep so you can run fast at the track meet tomorrow."

"Okay," said Jared. "Good night."

Your Turn

1. What worries you?
2. How can you allow God to be your shepherd?
3. How can God help you when you are afraid or nervous?

_____

_____

_____

_____

_____

_____

Prayer

Teach me to stay close to You, God. I want you to be my Shepherd. Amen.

TRACK AND FIELD DAY

Draw a line from each boy to the safety of the shepherd. Write your worries on the center lines.

GOD'S AWESOME CARE

I'm one of God's sheep.
The Lord is my shepherd, I shall not be in want.

Psalm 23:1

God Knows

"Jared, sheep don't worry about what will happen to them when they have a loving shepherd," said Mother. "Sheep are scared easily. A good shepherd makes sure his flock is safe from wild animals.

"Sheep need lots of green grass to eat. A good shepherd provides his sheep with dark green pastures. A good shepherd rubs oil on the nose of his sheep to keep flies away."

"My nose itches just hearing about it!" said Jared. "Can anyone be one of God's sheep?"

"Yes, God wants to be your Shepherd!" Mother replied. "Just ask Him to care for you and help you. Let's pray to your good Shepherd right now and ask Him for help."

Your Turn

1. Are there people in your life who pester you like flies pester sheep? Can you pray for them?
2. How can God your Shepherd keep the pests away from you?
3. Lambs sometimes go away from their flock and get lost. What can a lamb do to stay safe and out of trouble?
4. What can you do to stay safe and out of trouble?

_____

_____

_____

_____

_____

_____

Prayer

God, will You help me? I want You to be my Shepherd. Help me keep out of trouble and stay safe. Thank You for being my Shepherd. Amen.

PESKY FLIES

Write the name of a pest in your life on the line next to each fly. A pest can be worry, a bully, your own sin, etc.

GOD'S AWESOME CARE

God is my friend.
He was called God's friend.

James 2:23

A Friend Who Cares

Do you have a friend? Would you like to have a friend who cares? Most guys want to have at least one friend.

A friend is someone you like to spend time with. Friends trade baseball cards and baseball caps. A friend goes to birthday parties with you. Friends can make you laugh when you have a bad day. A friend talks to you and listens. You can tell a friend anything. A friend likes you no matter what you say and do. You can be silly, sad, quiet or loud around your friend. Your friend is always there.

Guy friends are nice to have, but God is the best friend to have. Moses was God's friend. Abraham was God's friend. God cared about them.

You can be one of God's friends, too. God is a friend who cares about you. He wants to hear from you each day. Your secrets are safe with God. He loves you at all times and in every way. Will you let Him be your best friend because He cares?

Your Turn

1. Do you have a friend? Who is your friend?
2. What does it mean to be a friend?
3. How can you be God's best friend?

_____

_____

_____

_____

_____

_____

Prayer

Thank You for being my friend, God. Teach me to be a good friend to others, too. Amen.

TRADING CARDS

Friends like to trade sports cards. If God is your best friend, what can you trade with Him? (love? time?) On the card below, make a special trading card for God by drawing a picture of something you can give Him. The other card shows what God wants to give you.

GOD'S AWESOME CARE

God's love for me is big.
So great is his love.

Psalm 103:11

Giant Love

"Dad, when will you get back from your trip?" asked Brett.

"I will return on Thursday," Dad said as he slid on his coat.

"Oh, that means you will be gone four days," replied Brett. "My game is Thursday night! I hope you get back in time to go."

"I do too, buddy!" said Dad. "I'll sure try. I don't like missing your football games. I know aunt Karen will take good care of you while I'm gone. Love you, buddy."

"Love you, too, Dad. See you Thursday," said Brett.

Has anyone told you, "I love you?" Did it make you happy inside? The words "I love you" are nice to hear.

How many ways does God say "I love you"? How often does God use those words in the Bible? Many times! He wants you to feel loved by Him. No matter what God is doing, He always loves you. Just like Brett's dad loved Brett, God loves you.

God's love is giant. It is bigger than the mountains. It is bigger than the ocean waters. It is bigger than the earth. His love is a big gift for you to have right now. Go and tell others that God's love is "giant."

Your Turn

1. How do you know that God loves you?
2. Have you ever told your family members you love them? Tell them now!
3. How can you tell God you love Him?

_____

_____

_____

_____

Prayer

God, I want to know Your love. Thank You for loving me. Teach me to love others. Amen.

GOD'S LOVE

Write "God Loves Me" on the big heart that covers the earth. Color the picture.

GOD'S AWESOME CARE

God has chosen you to know Him.
You did not choose Me, but I choose you.

John 15:16

God Chooses Me

Pick me! Pick me!

Have you ever been the last one to be picked for the team game? Did you ever wait in line all day for tickets to a special movie? You wait and wait, but the movie tickets are sold out before you can buy one.

Have you raised your hand in school ready to give a good answer? Then, the teacher calls on someone else?

There is someone who chooses you every time. He will never leave you out. There is someone who will let you talk to Him anytime. It is God! He wants to hear you and see you.

God doesn't make you wait to talk to Him. He never wants to leave you out. Just as God chose each star in the sky, God chose you. God loves you! Matthew 10:29 says, "Not one sparrow will fall to the ground without God knowing about it." He doesn't leave out the sparrows. He won't leave you out either.

Your Turn

1. Did you know God chooses you? What should you do about it?
2. How can you know God?
3. How should you treat others who aren't chosen for games at camp, school and other activities?

_____

_____

_____

_____

_____

_____

Prayer

Thank You, God, for choosing me. Thank You for making me feel loved by You. I am glad You chose me. Amen.

LEFT OUT

Draw yourself next to Jesus and in the center of the crowd of kids. Remember that God chose you and never wants to leave you out.

GOD'S AWESOME POWER

Nothing is impossible for God.
For nothing is impossible with God.

Luke 1:37

God Can Do Anything

One spring night enemy soldiers came into a little town. In a farm house near the town there lived a family. The young boy in the family often prayed to God. He believed that God could do anything.

When the soldiers came near, the boy prayed, "Dear God, please build a wall around this town. Protect us from the enemy soldiers."

The boy's father heard him pray. The father didn't believe in God.

"Your God can't build a wall around a whole town in one day and night," he said.

The next morning the family woke up to loud claps of thunder and high winds. Large hail also fell on the roof of their farm house. The father could hardly believe his eyes.

"Come here, son," he called to the young boy. "God has sent a heavy rain storm. The news reported that the storm is only over our town today. The rain has fallen so heavy that the soldiers have marched away from the town."

Now the father believed that God could do anything. He believed that God answers the prayers of His children.

When God wants to do something for you, you can't stop Him. God can do anything because His power is awesome.

Your Turn

1. Is there anything God can't do for you?
2. What kind of power does God have? What kind of things can He do?
3. When has God shown you His power?

_____

_____

_____

Prayer

Dear God, I'm glad You can do anything and that You answer my prayers. Help me to trust You to answer my prayers. I thank You for Your power that answers my prayers. Amen.

MY IMPOSSIBLE LIST

Think of three things you think are impossible for God to do for you. Write them on the giant rain drop below. Pray each day for them. Remember that God answers prayers with the best for you in mind. It may not be what you want, but it is the best.

IMPOSSIBLE LIST

1 _____

2 _____

3 _____

GOD'S AWESOME POWER

My God is holy.
God said, "Take off your sandals, for the place
where you are standing is holy ground."

Exodus 3:5

A Bush That Burns

In the flames of a bush fire an angel appeared to Moses. Moses saw fire coming from the bush. The fire looked very strange to Moses because the bush was not burning.

How can a bush burn, but not burn up? Moses thought.

When God saw Moses walking toward the bush He called out to him, "Moses!"

"I am here," said Moses.

"Don't come any closer!" God answered. "Take off your sandals! The place where you stand is holy," replied the Lord.

Moses took off his shoes and covered his face. He didn't want to look at God, even though God loved Moses. No one can look right at God because He is holy. The ground was made holy because God was there.

God told Moses about Himself at the bush. "I am who I am," said God. God meant that He is a holy and powerful God.

Your Turn

1. God presented Himself to Moses as a burning bush. How does God present Himself to you today?
2. What can you do now to show God you know He is Holy?
3. Why did God ask Moses to take off his shoes?

_____

_____

_____

_____

_____

Prayer

You are a holy God and I love You. I bow down to You and You alone. Amen.

THE BURNING BUSH

God showed Himself in a bush that burned. Moses took off His shoes because He knew God was holy. Draw your favorite shoes on the ground below the bush to remind you that God is holy.

GOD'S AWESOME POWER

God shows us He is Lord.
By this you will know that I am the Lord.

Exodus 7:17

My Walking Stick

"What if Mr. Wilson doesn't believe me?" Dave asked his mom. "What if he won't listen to me? He thinks I broke out his window."

Trying to prove something to someone who doesn't want to believe you is hard. Moses was sent to Egypt to talk to the king. God wanted him to tell the king to free the Jewish people. Moses had to show the people of Egypt that he was sent there by God and that God was powerful.

"What if the Jewish people and the king don't believe I spoke with You?" Moses asked God. "What if they won't listen to me? God, what if they say You never told me to come here?"

"What is that you hold in your hand?" asked God.

"My walking stick," said Moses.

"Throw it down," said God.

Moses obeyed God and threw his stick on the ground. It turned into a snake. Moses ran from the snake. God told Moses to reach out for it.

"Pick it up by its tail," said God. Moses reached out and grabbed the snake. It turned back into a walking stick.

"Do this and it will show the people that I sent you here," said God. "Take your walking stick and go Egypt."

Your Turn

1. Do you think you would believe God if you saw a stick turn into a snake in His name?
2. What are some ways God shows us His power today?

_____

_____

_____

_____

Prayer

God, help me to know You more each day. I pray I will see Your power even today. Amen.

GOD'S POWER SNAKE

How does God show us His power today? What do you see around you that shows God's power and might? Draw a picture below of one thing around you that shows God's power.

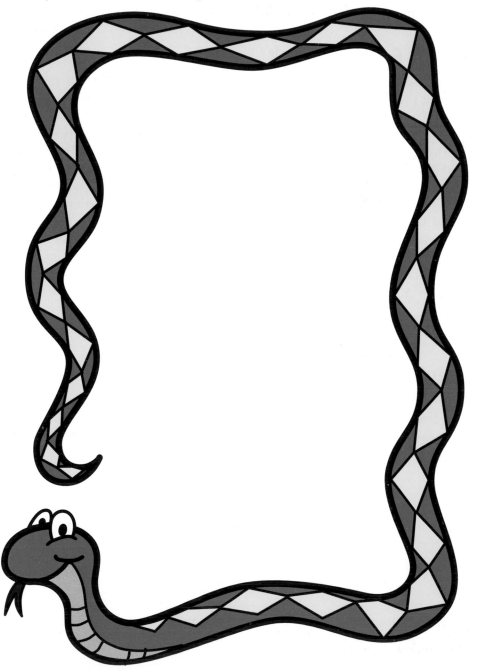

GOD'S AWESOME POWER

God uses His power to show He cares for you.
They will tell of the power of your awesome works.

Psalm 145:6

Water From A Rock

A radio uses electric power. A television takes electric power. An electric train set takes power. A telephone works with power. All of these things run by manmade power.

Did you know that God is all powerful? God has the power to do anything. The Bible tells true stories about how God used His power to help people.

One time God's people were traveling in the desert. The people had nothing to drink. They were very thirsty and they didn't know what to do. Moses was their leader, so he cried out to God, "What am I going to do? These people are thirsty. If I don't find drink for them they will kill me."

God told Moses to take his walking stick and go on ahead of the people. "I'll stand by the rock at Horeb," said God. "Moses, you hit the rock and water will come flowing from the rock. Then my people can take a drink."

Then the people knew God was taking care of them. God still shows His powerful care for us today.

Your Turn

1. How is God's power different than man's power? Does God show His power to us today?
2. Can you think of any other stories in the Bible where God showed His power and care for people?

_____

_____

_____

_____

Prayer

Dear God, thank You for Your power and might. Let me know You more as I see Your power in the Bible and my life.

THE ROCK

Water flowed out of the rock for Moses and the people. God showed He cared for them by sending water. Think of two ways God shows He cares for you. Write them on the rock. Do you see His power as He cares for you?

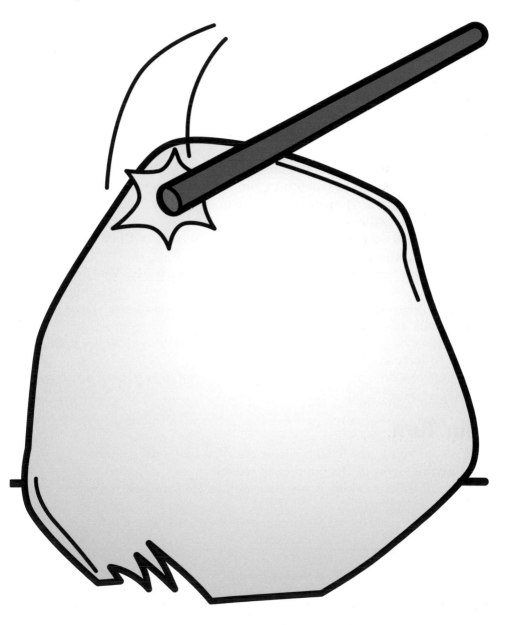

GOD'S AWESOME POWER

God wants you close to Him.
Let us draw near to God with a sincere heart.
Hebrews 10:22

A Friend's Back

Has anyone told you not to look directly at the sun? Looking at the sun without sunglasses can harm your eyes. The sun is always there shining down on you to keep you warm. Even when it is cloudy, the sun is there behind the clouds.

That is kind of the way it is with God. God is always with you to care for you. God is so holy that you couldn't look right at His face. Even Moses, a man who loved God, couldn't look at God's face.

Moses asked God to teach him His ways. Moses wanted to know God as a friend. "Please, show me who You are. Show me Your greatness," said Moses.

God told Moses, "I'll tell you more about Myself, but I can't let you see My face. Anyone who sees my face will die."

Then God said, "You can stand on a rock beside Me. My goodness will pass by you. As I pass by I will put you in a dent in the rock. I'll place My hand over you. After I pass by, I'll move My hand off of you. Then you will see My back and not My face."

That is what happened to Moses. He saw God's back! Moses is the only person to have ever been that close to God.

When you draw near to God, He draws near to you. God wants you to be as close as a friend.

Your Turn

1. How do you make friends? How can you be God's friend?
2. Why did God put His hand over Moses?
3. Do you think God loves you as much as He loved Moses?

_____

_____

_____

Prayer

God, I want to be Your child and Your friend. Please draw near to me like You did Moses. I want to know You! Amen.

THE DENT

Draw yourself in the dent of the rock below to remind you God wants to be near you. Write the Scripture from Hebrews 10:22 below the cave.

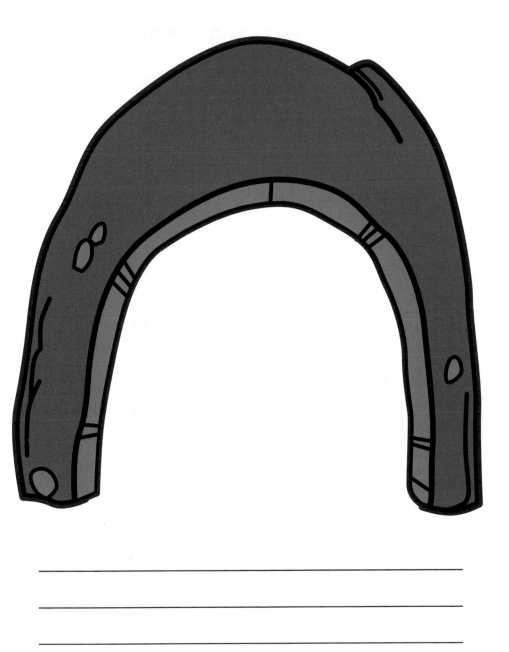

GOD'S AWESOME POWER

I will learn to trust God in everything.
I have trusted in the Lord without wavering.

Psalm 26:1

The Ax and Knife

Jamie and his dad liked to fish at the pond near their house. Once Jamie reached out to put a worm on his hook. As he bent over, his fishing knife slid out of his shirt pocket and into the water. He looked down to see if it would float to the top.

"Dad, my knife is in the pond," he said. "Will it float to the top so I can get it again?"

"No!" said dad. "It is too heavy to float to the top of the water. Let's pray and maybe Jesus will help us find it with this net."

Once in Bible times many men were cutting down trees at the river. They were building a new place to worship God. As one man cut with an ax, the sharp end of the ax flew off. The ax ended up in the river.

"Oh no!" cried the man. "That ax isn't mine! It belongs to someone else and I must find it."

The men called out to Elisha, a man of God. "Come and help us find the ax."

Elisha cut a stick and threw it into the water. It landed right where the ax had fallen in. Suddenly, the iron ax rested on top of the water.

"Lift it out!" said Elisha. The man picked it out of the water.

Elisha showed the man that God cared about his losing an ax. Put your trust in God because He cares for you. God may not always do what you want Him to, but He knows what is right.

Your Turn

1. Why did the man ask Elisha to help him find the ax?
2. Have you ever prayed and asked God and Jesus to help you find something that is lost?
3. How can you help others learn to trust in God and Jesus?

_____

_____

Prayer

Dear God help me to trust You for everything. I know I don't always think about asking You for help. I pray I will think of You when I lose something or need help. Amen.

A TRUSTED AX

On the axhead write what you can trust God for in your life. Color the handle.

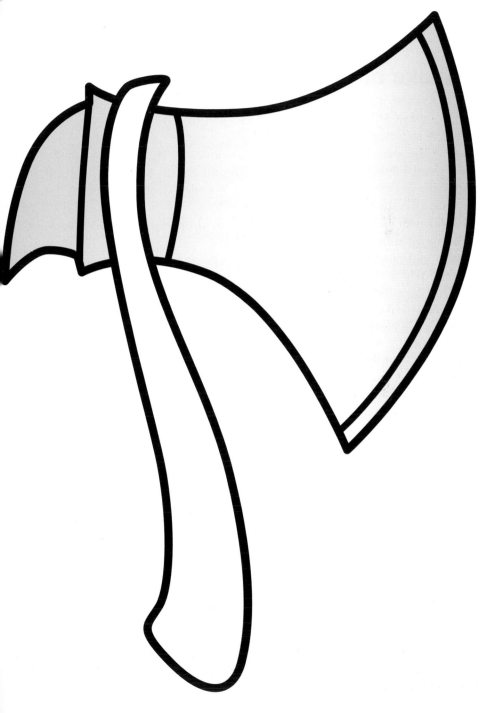

GOD'S AWESOME POWER

God forgives me when I do wrong.
*If we confess our sins, He is faithful
and just to forgive us our sins.*
1 John 1:9

A Snake on a Pole

Moses led many of God's people out of Egypt so they could get away from a mean king. God promised He would care for His people as they traveled to a new land.

But the people didn't honor God's love for them. They fussed about everything. The people began to say mean things to Moses.

"Why did you bring us here?" they asked. "There's no bread to eat and we hate this food. We will die out here!"

God was sad, so He sent snakes into their camp. The snakes bit the people and some died.

The people called out to Moses. "We have sinned against God with our fussing. We have been selfish and unkind to you, Moses."

The people cried to Moses, "Pray to God and ask Him to take the snakes away from us."

Moses prayed to God. God told Moses to make a metal snake and place it on a pole.

"People who get a snake bite can look at the pole and they won't die," said God.

The people went to the pole and asked God to forgive them. God loved them so much that He forgave them. God's people learned a lesson about fussing and selfishness. They also learned that when you say you are sorry and you mean it, God forgives you.

Your Turn

1. Why did God send snakes into His people's camp?
2. Were the people really sorry they fussed? How did God show them His forgiveness?
3. Will God forgive you for everything?

Prayer

Dear God, teach me not to fuss when I don't get my way. I thank You for Your love and forgiveness. You are a good and loving God. You teach me many good things. Amen.

MY POLE

Draw a snake around the pole below. Write what you need God to forgive you for. Pray and ask God to forgive you now.

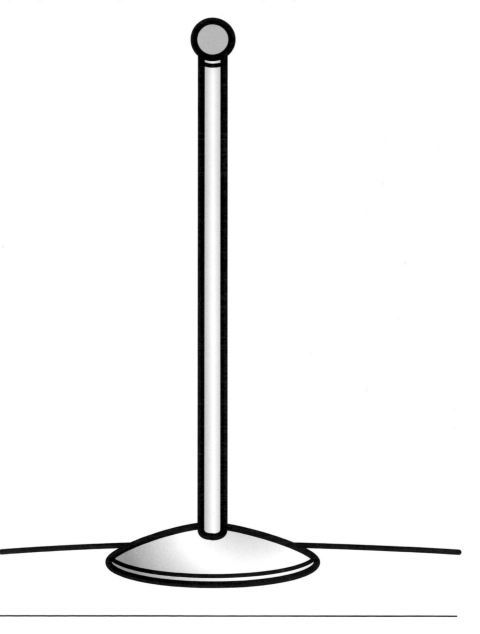

_____

_____

_____

GOD'S AWESOME POWER

I will do what God tells me to do.
Go near and listen to all that the Lord our God says.
Deuteronomy 5:27

A Donkey Who Talks, Part One

There was a king who ruled over a place called Moab. He was afraid of God's people. He heard that God helped them in battles to take over land.

The people of Moab said, "God's people will eat us like an ox eats grass." So the king of Moab sent his helpers to get a man named Balaam.

If Balaam prays for bad things to happen to God's people, then I can fight and win, he thought. *Maybe then they will leave my land.*

Even though Balaam prayed, he didn't know the one true God. God knew him, but he didn't know God.

The king's men asked him to go with them to Moab and pray bad things for God's people. God came to Balaam and told him not to go with the men.

"You'd better not pray for bad things to happen to My people," said God. "They are made special by Me and I want them to have good things."

Balaam told the men to go back home. "God won't let me go with you," he said.

More men were sent by the king to talk to Balaam. They told Balaam that the king would pay him silver and gold if he came with them.

So God came to Balaam that night. "You can go with the men," God said, "but do only what I tell you."

Balaam acted like he knew God and wanted to obey Him. God knew Balaam didn't really want to obey Him. The next day Balaam got on his donkey and went with the kings' men. Read the next devotion to find out what happened to Balaam.

Your Turn

1. Do you think Balaam really wanted to obey God or did he just act like he wanted to?
2. Is God more concerned that we obey or that we want to obey?

Prayer

God, I pray You will help me to obey my parents and want to. I ask that You give me the desire to please them and You. Amen.

BALAAM'S FACES

Balaam listened to God, but didn't really desire to obey Him. Color the face that would please God the most. The answer is on page 229.

1. Balaam doesn't want to listen to God or obey God.

2. Balaam doesn't want to listen to God, but he will obey Him.

3. Balaam wants to listen to God and obey Him.

GOD'S AWESOME POWER

I will listen to God and obey Him.
We will listen and obey.

Deuteronomy 5:27

A Donkey Who Talks 2

Balaam rode his donkey with the men to see the king of Moab. God became upset with Balaam. He knew Balaam's heart was really against Him. God sent an angel holding a sword to stand in the road. Only the donkey could see God's angel. The donkey was afraid and ran. Balaam was mean to the donkey and hit her.

The road became narrow and twisted between walls. The angel appeared again! The donkey saw the angel and moved close to the wall. Balaam's leg hit the wall, so Balaam hit the donkey.

Surprisingly, God made the donkey talk. "Why do you hit me so much?"

"You made me look foolish," said Balaam.

"But I am your very own donkey! You ride me all the time," said the donkey.

Then God made Balaam able to see the angel. Balaam put his face on the ground. "I have sinned," he said. "Should I go home?"

"Go with the men," said the angel. "But say only what God tells you to say."

Balaam went to the king's house. He told the king that he could not pray bad things for God's people.

"God has not planned bad things for them," he said. "I will only say what God tells me to say. A very special person will come from these people. He will be like a star and will win over His enemy."

Balaam gave up the silver and gold to listen to God and obey Him.

Your Turn

1. Why do you think the donkey was able to see the angel, but Balaam was not able to see her?
2. Why do you think God made the donkey talk? If God can make a donkey talk, what else can God do?
3. Who is the special person Balaam talked about as being like a star?

_____

_____

Prayer

Dear God, help me to understand Your words in the Bible. Let me listen to You and hear Your voice. Help me to obey You! Amen.

DONKEY TALK

Balaam's heart wasn't ready to understand the things of God. Do you have questions about God? Write your question under the donkey's feet. Ask your mom or dad to help you find the answers. God will help you understand His ways.

_____

_____

_____

GOD'S AWESOME POWER

I can be in God's army.
Commit your way to the Lord; trust in him.

Psalm 37:5

Strong Walls Fall

"Keep the gates closed!" they shouted.

The people of Jericho wanted to keep others out of their city. But God had a different plan! He wanted Jericho to be a place where God is loved.

God told Joshua, "I am going to let you and your people have Jericho. Have your army march around the city. March one time each day for six days. "On the seventh day, march seven times around the city walls. Let the guards and ministers go in front and blow their horns on that day. When my people hear the horns, they should shout as loud as they can. The city walls will fall down as they shout."

Joshua's people marched on the first day. Then they went back to their camp for the night. The next morning they got up and marched again. Each day for six days they marched.

Day seven finally came. Joshua's army marched again, but this time they marched seven times. The ministers made a long sound on their horns. Joshua called out, "Everyone shout! God is giving us the city."

The horns blew and the people shouted! The tall walls of the city came falling down. Joshua and his army went right into the city. The city now belonged to God's people.

God wants you to be like Joshua's army. Pray that your city will belong to God and His people. Tell others about Jesus.

Your Turn

1. How can you be in God's army at home and at school?
2. Name two ways you can win your city for God.

_____

_____

_____

_____

Prayer

Dear God, I pray my city will know You. I pray You will help me tell others about You and Jesus. Help my friends and neighbors to know You. Amen.

CITY WALLS

Draw a picture on the city wall that shows ways to win your city for God. Write the name of your city on the wall.

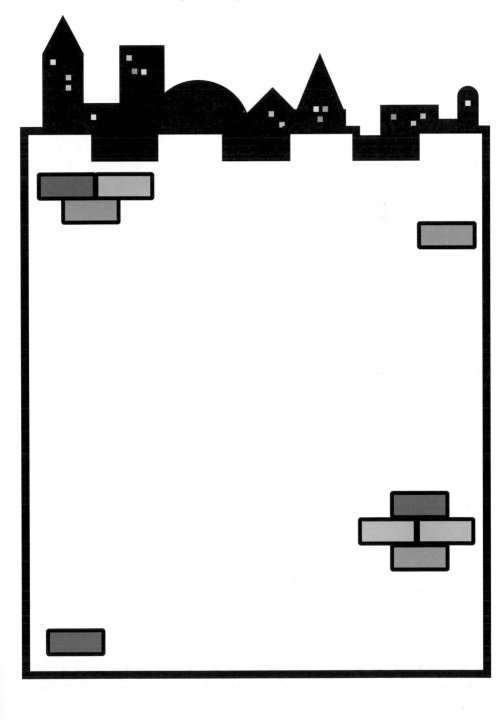

GOD'S AWESOME POWER

I can tell others of God's wonders.
Sing praise to him; tell of all his wonderful acts.

Psalm 105:2

The Sun and Moon Stand Still

Imagine fighting five king's armies in one battle! That is just what God's army had to do.

They were led by Joshua. God told Joshua, "Don't be afraid. I'll help you win."

Joshua's army marched all night to surprise the king's armies. God made the king's armies confused, so they ran. Big hail stones fell from the sky. God's army chased the king's armies. The hail fell right on the heads of the enemy.

Joshua prayed to God, "Let the sun stand still." The sun stood still and the moon stopped moving too. The sun didn't move for one whole day. That gave God's army more daylight to fight and win.

God's people took all the land that day. The Bible tells about many powerful acts of God. Knowing about God's powerful acts shows who He is.

You should tell others about your wonderful God. His power helps you and shows you His love. Can you see His power today?

Your Turn

1. Who can you tell about God's wonderful power?
2. How does God show His power today?
3. Do you believe God can do anything?

Prayer

Dear God You are powerful and kind. Thank You for caring about me and using Your power to show love to me. Amen.

GOD'S WONDERS

Write on the sun and moon some ways God shows His power.

GOD'S AWESOME POWER

God gives me strength to do many things.
It is God who arms me with strength.

Psalm 18:32

A Donkey's Jaw Bone

"What makes you so strong?" the people asked Samson. But it was a secret! Samson wouldn't tell anyone.

Samson was special to God from the time he was born. He was very strong. His strength came from God. God had always told him not to cut off his hair.

"If you cut your hair, you won't be the strongest man anymore," said God.

Samson made many enemies because he had a bad temper. God wasn't pleased with his temper, but He stilled loved him.

One day a huge army of men went after Samson to hurt him. Some men tied him up with ropes. The army began to shout and charge toward him.

The spirit of God helped Samson by giving him great strength. The rope couldn't keep him tied anymore.

Samson broke the rope and picked up a jaw bone from a dead donkey. He began to fight the men with the jaw bone. He killed 1,000 men. People decided to call that place "Jaw Bone Hill."

Where do you get strength to take a hard spelling test at school? Do you ask God to help you with chores and other hard jobs? God wants to help you in all you do. Count on Him!

Your Turn

1. Where does your strength come from? Do you ever try to be strong without God's help?
2. God wants us to count on Him for strength, like Samson did. What does God tell us about what He will do (see the Scripture above)?

_____

_____

Prayer

Dear God, help me to count on You. Show me how to trust in You to help me when doing something is difficult. Let me help others learn to count on You, too. Amen.

THE JAW BONE

On the donkey's jaw bone below, list something you need God's strength to do (like obey your parents).

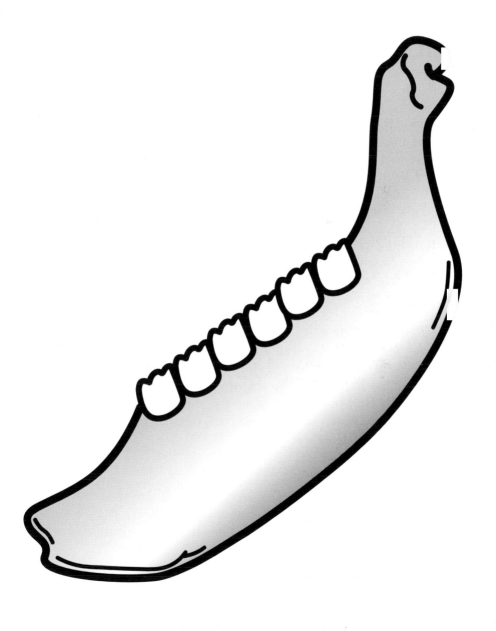

GOD'S AWESOME POWER

I remember when God has helped me.
My help comes from the Lord, the Maker of heaven and earth.
Psalm 121:2

A Fight With Thunder

"Will you love God more than your favorite ranger action figure? Will you love God more than a video game?" asked Pastor Hinds.

Pat sat and listened as his children's pastor spoke to him and his friends. Pastor Hinds made the Bible sound awesome.

Pat remembered a story his pastor told about a fight with thunder. He told how Samuel, God's prophet, talked to the people of Israel. Samuel told them to love and serve only God. Then Samuel called all of the people together in one place. "I'll pray to God for you," he said.

The people fasted that day and confessed their sins to God. They told God, "We've done wrong and have sinned." The people's enemies heard that the Israelites were together in one place. So they came to fight them.

God's people were afraid. "Keep praying for us, Samuel," they said. "We need God to help us."

The enemies moved closer and closer. Samuel prayed more and more. Suddenly, God spoke in a loud voice. The sound of His voice was like a clap of thunder in a storm.

The enemies were so scared that they ran right into God's people. God's people went out to fight and they won.

Samuel was so happy that he set up a stone. He called it "The Help Stone." He said, "God has helped us so far." God's people knew they had sinned against God. When they turned back to God, He forgave them and helped them.

Your Turn

1. What does God do when we are sorry for doing wrong?
2. What does God do when we draw near to Him?
3. Can you remember times when God has helped you? Did you thank God?
4. Do you think God would help you like He helped Samuel and the people?

Prayer

Thank You for loving me and helping me when I turn to You for help. Help me to love You more than anything. Amen.

THE HELPING STONE

Do you remember the last time God helped you? Color your own Helping Stone below. Write on the rock those things God does to help you.

GOD'S AWESOME POWER

God wants to rule over my life.
He rules forever by His power.

Psalm 66:7

The Writing Fingers

Jason was a daydreamer at school. He stared at the chalkboard. He looked as if he was hearing Mrs. Pack's math lesson, but he wasn't listening at all.

He daydreamed about a Bible story he heard. The story was about a king who thought he was more important than God. He built statues of himself and made the people worship him, not God. God wanted to rule over the king's life, but the king wouldn't let Him.

One night the king invited many people to eat dinner with him. As they ate and drank, something happened! Suddenly, a man's fingers appeared by the wall. The fingers began writing something.

The king was scared at what he saw. His face went white. His knees were shaking. The king called in magicians.

"What does it say?" asked the king. None of the men could read the writing. Then the queen said, "I know of a very wise man named Daniel. Many things are known and understood by this man. Surely he can tell you what is written on the wall."

Daniel was called in. He looked at the wall and saw the words: MENE, MENE, TEKEL, PARSIN.

"Read the wall for me," said the king.

Daniel began, "MENE means God will end your days as king. TEKEL means you've been tested by God and shown that you don't love Him. PARSIN means two nations will share your land."

That very night the king died and Daniel was made an important man in the kingdom. Unlike the king, Daniel let God rule his life!

Your Turn

1. What does it mean to let God rule in your life?
2. Why couldn't the magic men read the writings?

Prayer

Dear God, I want You to rule in my life. Help me to say yes to You and no to sin. Amen.

A CHALKBOARD MESSAGE

God sent a message to the king. He wanted to get his attention. Decode the message below. What does God want to say to you? The answer is on page 229.

a	b	c	d	e	f	g	h	i
1	2	3	4	5	6	7	8	9

j	k	l	m	n	o	p	q	r
10	11	12	13	14	15	16	17	18

s	t	u	v	w	x	y	z
19	20	21	22	23	24	25	26

___ ___ ___   ___ ___ ___ ___ ___
7 15 4   18 21 12 5 19

___ ___ ___ ___   ___ ___ .
15 22 5 18   13 5

GOD'S AWESOME POWER

God hears my prayers.
He hears the prayers of the righteous.

Proverbs 15:29

A Shadow Moves Backward

Have you heard of the groundhog and his shadow? It is believed that he comes out of his den each February 3rd. If when he comes out he does not see his shadow, that is a sign that spring will come early. If he does see his shadow, that is a sign of six more weeks of winter.

The story of the groundhog is just a tale. The Bible tells a true story about a shadow sent as a sign to a king. King Hezekiah was sick and dying. He prayed to God and asked Him for healing.

Hezekiah cried out to God, "Remember I have done what is right and I have obeyed You. I obeyed You even when the people didn't like what I did."

God heard Hezekiah's cries. He healed him! God told Hezekiah He would let him live for 15 more years. He would also save his city from enemy hands.

God sent a sign to the king to show him He would answer his prayer. The sign was a shadow on the stairs. God didn't just make the shadow move on the stairs. God made the shadow move 10 steps backward on the stairs!

God's power is awesome. He heard the king's prayers. He will hear your prayers, too.

Your Turn

1. Why did God answer Hezekiah's prayers?
2. Can you think of a neighbor or friend you can pray for now?

_____

_____

_____

_____

_____

Prayer

Thank You, God, for hearing my prayers. I pray You will remind me to pray for others. Amen.

PRAYER SHADOWS

God sent a shadow to Hezekiah as a sign of God's faithfulness. Write three prayers inside the stairs below. As God answers your prayers, record them at the bottom of the page.

GOD'S AWESOME POWER

There is nothing God can't do.
I am the Lord, the God of all mankind.
Is anything too hard for me?

Jeremiah 32:26

God's Special Mailman

"The mailman is here, Dad," said James. "I'll go get it."

James found a postcard from his grandpa and grandma in the mailbox. "I hope there is good news from them," he said.

Do you like getting good messages from people? The Bible tells about a woman named Mary. Mary got a good message from God's special mailman. God sent the angel Gabriel with a message for Mary. It wasn't a written message. It was a message of words from God.

"Hello!" said Gabriel to Mary. "God is with you! He loves you and you belong to Him."

Mary didn't know what to do. She was so afraid!

"Don't be afraid," said Gabriel. "You are going to have a baby boy. You will name Him Jesus. He will be great and rule over all of God's people. His kingdom will last forever."

How can this be? she thought. I am not even married. Mary was engaged to marry a man named Joseph, but they weren't married yet.

"God's power will come over you like a shadow," said Gabriel. "The baby will be very special because He will be God's Son."

Mary answered the angel of God. "I want to serve God, so let this happen to me. God is great! My spirit is happy with God."

This message to Mary was greater than any message sent to anyone.

Your Turn

1. Why do you think this message to Mary was so important?
2. Do you think Mary was happy about the message? Why or why not?

_____

_____

_____

Prayer

Dear God, I thank You for the message about Jesus. Thank You for Your power. Thank You for sending Jesus to rule over us and love us. Amen.

MAIL FOR GOD

Mary's message back to God told Him how great He was. Draw a picture message to God telling Him thank You for His power.

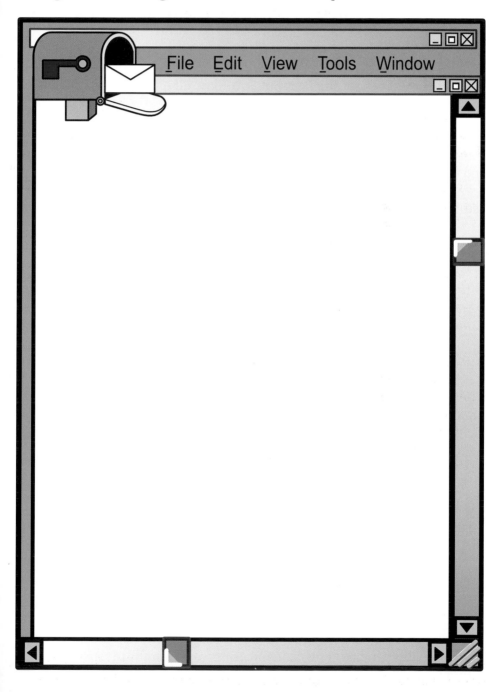

GOD'S AWESOME POWER

I can feel safe knowing Jesus.
He will keep me safe in his dwelling.

Psalm 27:5

The Roaring Storm

"Hey, Ray! Let's get the boat out Saturday. I'll take you for a ride on the lake," said Uncle Carl.

"Are you sure it won't storm?" asked Ray. "I get afraid on the lake in storms. Do you remember the storm the last time we went out?"

"I sure do, Ray! But, we will watch the weather report and trust God. God will go with us and keep us safe," said Uncle Carl.

A few minutes later, Uncle Carl said, "Ray! Have you heard the story of a storm in the Bible? Jesus and His friends got into a boat to cross the lake. A roaring storm blew in on them. The waves crashed over and around the boat. Lightening flashed all around. Water almost filled the boat. The whole time Jesus laid in back sleeping."

"Wow," said Ray. "I couldn't sleep like that. I would be scared!"

"Well, Jesus' friends were so scared that they woke Jesus up," said Uncle Carl. "Jesus got up and spoke right to the storm."

"What did He say?" asked Ray.

" 'Be quiet! Just be still!' Then the wind died down and everything was still. This time Jesus' friends were scared again. But they were afraid of what Jesus did.

"They looked at each other. 'Who is this man Jesus?' they asked each other. 'The winds and the rain obey Him.' "

"Wow," said Ray. "I guess they didn't know how safe they were with Jesus there. I want to feel safe with Jesus."

"You can!" said Uncle Carl. "Let's pray about that right now!"

Your Turn

1. What things keep you from feeling safe?
2. How can Jesus help you feel safe?

Prayer

Dear Jesus, help me to know You and Your ways. I want to trust You more. Help me to tell my friends that they can trust You, too. Amen.

A SAFE BOAT

Draw a picture of your friends in the boat with you and Jesus.

He will keep me safe in his dwelling.
Psalm 27:5

GOD'S AWESOME POWER

I see power in God's love.
Show the wonders of your great love.

Psalm 17:7

The Sick Girl

Have you ever had to go home sick from school? Have you been in the hospital? Your parents worry about you when you are sick.

The Bible tells of a little girl who was so sick that she died. Many doctors had tried to make her well. Her father's name was Jairus. He was a leader in the town.

Jairus pushed through a crowd of people to get to Jesus. He bowed in front of Him.

My little girl is sick," he said. "She will die! Please come with me and touch her."

Jesus loved the little girl and her father. He went with Jairus. Friends came outside to greet them.

They said, "Your little girl is dead." Jairus cried in his hands.

Jesus said to Jairus, "Don't be afraid. Believe in Me. The Father in heaven will heal your child."

The girl's family was sobbing for her. "The girl is only asleep," said Jesus. He took the girl's hand and said, "My child, get up." At once she stood up. Jairus hugged and kissed his little girl.

Jesus healed the girl with the power of God's love. Do you know the power of God's love?

Your Turn

1. How does God feel when you are sick?
2. Does God love all people or just those that love Him?

_____

_____

_____

_____

Prayer

Thank You, God, for caring for me and loving me. Thank You for Your healing power. Amen.

LOVE PRINTS

Color the love footprints from your house all the way to God's house in heaven.

GOD'S AWESOME POWER

God wants me to share with others.
Do not forget to do good and share with others.
Hebrews 13:16

A Shared Lunch

"Hey! What do you have in your lunch sack today, Jeff?" asked Jared. "I left mine in the car pool car."

"I can give you an apple!" said Jeff.

"What about that candy bar?" asked Jared.

"No way!" snapped Jeff. "That's my favorite!"

"You wouldn't have been much help to Jesus," said Jared.

"What do you mean?" asked Jeff.

"I mean, a boy once shared his lunch with Jesus," said Jared. Then Jared told Jeff this story:

Jesus went up on the side of a mountain. He saw a crowd of people walking toward Him. Philip and Andrew stood by as the people neared.

"Where will we get food for these people?" He asked Philip. "We need lots of food. We would have to work for eight months to buy food for so many." Andrew spoke up. "Here is a boy who brought his own lunch. He has five rolls of bread and two fish."

"But that won't feed this big crowd!" said the friends.

Jesus told the men to sit the crowd in the grass. He took the five bread rolls and thanked God. Then He gave out all of the rolls. He took the fish and did the same thing. All of a sudden there were enough rolls and fish for every person there. Stomachs were full!

"Well, if that boy can share his lunch I guess I can too," said Jeff. "Let's share the candy bar with the whole lunch table."

I wonder if there is enough to go around the table? thought Jared.

Your Turn

1. How was Jesus able to make a little boy's lunch feed so many people?
2. How can sharing even small things like a lunch make others happy?

_____

_____

Prayer

Dear God, help me to share with others. Show me ways I can share at home and help my family. Amen.

TALL SHARING SANDWICH

Make a sharing sandwich! Draw or write on each part of the sandwich things you can share with family and friends.

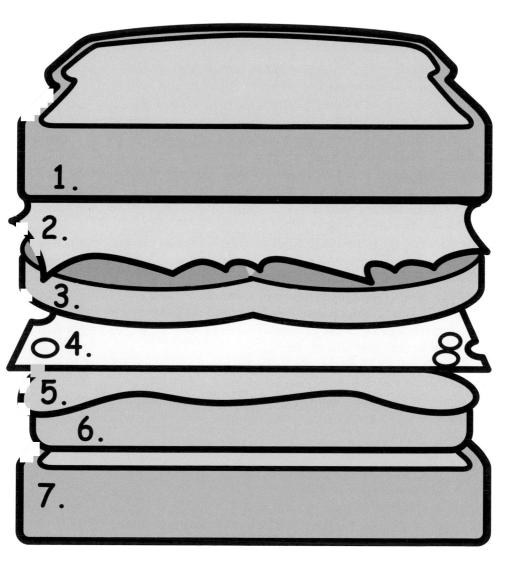

GOD'S AWESOME POWER

Jesus wants me to trust in Him.
Trust in the Lord with all your heart.

Proverbs 3:5

Water Shoes

Water skiing is fun! A water ski is a shoe you wear to slide along the water. When you water ski you wear a life jacket and hold onto a rope that is tied to the back of a boat. As the boat moves, the rope pulls you up and out of the water. You slide along the top of the water in your water shoes. You must trust the boat and the water skis to keep you on top of the water.

Jesus' friend Peter learned to trust Him, not a boat or water skis. Jesus had left a crowd to go into the hills to pray. He sent His special friends out in a boat. It was dark on the lake. A strong wind blew in. From the hills, Jesus saw His friends rowing hard. They tried to move the boat, but the wind blew it the other way!

Jesus went out to them. He walked right on top of the water! His friends saw Him coming but they were afraid because they thought He was a ghost.

"Don't be afraid!" said Jesus. "It is just me."

Then Jesus asked Peter to get out of the boat.

"Come to me!" said Jesus. Peter got out of the boat and stepped onto the water. He began to walk to Jesus. But as he saw the waves he got scared. He started to sink into the water.

"Lord, save me!" Peter cried. Jesus reached out and lifted him from the water.

"Your faith is small!" said Jesus. They both climbed into the boat.

Jesus doesn't want you to walk on water. He wants you to trust Him to love and care for you.

Your Turn

1. Why did Peter start to sink?
2. How can you trust God to help you at school?
3. Do you trust Jesus to help you when you are sad or angry? Do you ever "sink" like Peter?

Prayer

Dear God, help me to trust You at home and at school. Teach me how to keep my eyes on You. Amen.

TRUST LINE

Draw a line that leads from the boy to Jesus. On the line write things for which you can trust Jesus.

I will trust Jesus.

GOD'S AWESOME POWER

Big things can happen when I pray.
Whatever you ask for in prayer, believe and it will be yours.
Mark 11:24

PUSH for Peter

What if your friend was in jail for loving Jesus? There are families in far away places who go to jail for loving Jesus.

The Bible tells about a man named Peter who went to jail for loving Jesus. Peter faced death for following Jesus. Peter's friends were worried about him. They began to pray for Peter to be set free.

Peters friends Prayed Until Something Happened (PUSH)! God listened and answered their prayers in a powerful way.

God made His move in the middle of the night. A man appeared in Peter's cell. The chains on his arms and legs suddenly broke off.

"Put on your shoes," said the man. "Hurry! Wrap your coat around yourself."

The jail door swung open. Peter and the man walked out of the jail. Peter looked around, but the man was quickly gone. Peter went to a friend's house and stayed there until it was safe. His friends were so happy to see him! God had answered their prayers in a great way. Do you PUSH (Pray Until Something Happens)? That is just what Peter's friends did.

Your Turn

1. Do you believe God answers your prayers?
2. Do you ever PUSH?
3. Can you think of someone who needs your prayers now?

_____

_____

_____

_____

_____

_____

Prayer

Dear God, I pray for _____. Amen.

THE WHEELBARROW

Write more prayer requests in the wheelbarrow below. Begin PUSHing and praying. Watch God answer your prayers!

1. _____

   _____

2. _____

   _____

GOD'S AWESOME POWER

Jesus surprises me with His presence.
Set me in your presence forever.

Psalm 41:12

Surprised Friends

"Grandma and Grandpa, what a surprise!" said John. "I didn't know you were coming."

"We wanted to surprise you at your birthday party," said Grandma.

Jesus surprised His friends once. One night Peter and some guys were together. They got into a boat and went out on the lake to fish. They fished all night, but didn't catch anything.

Morning came and Jesus was standing on the shore. The men in the boat didn't guess it was Jesus because He had already gone to heaven.

"Don't you have any fish, My friends?" Jesus called. "No," they shouted back.

"Throw your net into the water on the right side of the boat. You'll find some fish there," said Jesus.

They threw their net over the right side of the boat. They caught many fish in the net! The net was so heavy the men couldn't lift it! Peter counted 153 fish. The net didn't even break.

There was a camp fire when they got to shore. They were very surprised to see that Jesus was there.

"Have breakfast!" said Jesus. Jesus' presence and the 153 fish had surprised His friends.

Jesus can surprise you, too! He can be near when you don't look for Him.

Your Turn

1. How did Jesus surprise His friends with His presence?
2. How does Jesus surprise you with His presence?
3. Write some places where Jesus might surprise you with His presence.

_____

_____

_____

Prayer

Thank You, Lord, for Your presence. I want to be near You. Being near You makes me happy. It makes You happy too! When You are near me I can do more things for You. Amen.

THE FISH NET

Draw a line to connect the fish in the net at the right of the boat.
Remember, Jesus surprises you with His presence.

GOD'S AWESOME POWER

I can tell my friends about Jesus.
Go into all the world and preach [tell] *the good news.*
Mark 16:15

In The Clouds

"Look at that cloud!" said Jason.

"It looks like a dragon," called Cory.

"Oh! Look at that one! It moves like a T-Rex dinosaur," shouted Jason.

"Just think," said Cory. "When Jesus left this earth, He went up in a cloud."

Jesus led His friends to a place called Bethany. He lifted up His hands to the sky. He prayed God would send goodness and happiness to them.

Then Jesus said, "Father God has planned many things for His people. He is in charge of all things. The Holy Spirit will come when I leave. The Holy Spirit will help you tell people about Me."

Suddenly, Jesus went up and off the ground. His friends watched until a cloud hid Him. Their eyes peered upward to the sky.

Then two men appeared next to them. The men were dressed in all white. "Friends of Jesus!" said the two men. "Why are you just standing here? Why are you looking at the sky? Jesus has gone up into heaven. Some day He will come back the same way you saw Him go."

Jesus' friends worshipped Him and left. Their hearts were full of love for God and Jesus. They went to the house of worship to pray for many hours.

Your Turn

1. How would you feel if you saw Jesus going into a cloud?
2. Who were the men who appeared in white clothes?
3. What did Jesus tell us to do before He went to heaven?

_____

_____

_____

Prayer

Dear Jesus, help me to share Your love with everyone I know. Help me to pray about people who don't know You. Amen.

CLOUD DRAWINGS

Think of someone who doesn't know Jesus. Draw a picture of him or her on the cloud.

GOD'S AWESOME POWER

Meeting Jesus changes me.
If anyone is in Christ he is a new creation.

2 Corinthians 5:17

A Meeting With Jesus

Have you met someone so nice and kind that you wanted to be like him or her? A man named Saul met someone like that on a road.

Saul planned to hurt followers of Jesus. He had hate in his heart for them. He wanted people who loved Jesus to go to jail.

Saul headed for a town called Damascus. He hoped to make trouble for Jesus' people.

All of a sudden, a bright light came from heaven. It shone all around him. Saul fell to the ground.

"Saul, Saul, why do you hurt Me?" a voice called.

"Who are you?" asked Saul.

"I'm Jesus," said the voice. "I'm the one you are hurting. Get up! Go to Damascus."

Saul got on his feet and opened his eyes. But he couldn't see anything. A friend took his hand and led him into the city. God sent a man to pray for him. The man put his hands on Saul. Saul's hate for Jesus' followers turned to love. Right away, a thin cover fell off Saul's eyes. He could see again! God's Holy Spirit filled him.

Saul became very powerful for Jesus. Meeting Jesus changed him. Saul got up and began telling everyone about Jesus.

Your Turn

1. Jesus met Saul on the road. Where can He meet you?
2. What made Saul stop hating followers of Jesus?
3. How would someone be different after meeting Jesus?

_____

_____

_____

Prayer

Show me ways I can meet You and love You. Help me to love others. Help me to love kids who are mean and unkind to me. Show me how to help others meet you. Amen.

MEET JESUS ON THE ROAD

Meet Jesus on your road! Draw yourself next to Jesus to show you have met Him. Write your name on the road sign.

GOD'S AWESOME RULES

God has rules for me to follow.
Obey the Lord your God and carefully follow all his commands.
Deuteronomy 28:1

God's Rules!

On the first day of school as Mr. Clark gave the classroom rules, Phil listened carefully.

The same rules, he thought. Every year I hear the same rules.

"Rules are very important," said Mr. Clark. "Some rules are made so games will be fun and interesting. Other rules are made to show respect for others."

"In soccer," Mr. Clark continued, "there is a rule that you can't touch the ball with your hands. That makes the game fun! In basketball, no pushing or shoving is allowed. That rule shows respect for others."

A football rule says you can't pull on the front of a players helmet. "It's easy to see the reason for that rule!" said Mr. Clark.

Rules are made for many good reasons. They help us to keep ourselves and others safe. Some rules are created to make life easier. Phil knew Mr. Clark was right. God also gives us rules to follow.

God's rules keep us safe and show us when we are doing wrong in His eyes. Doing wrong in God's eyes is sin. We call God's rules "The Ten Commandments." They are listed in the Old Testament of the Bible in Exodus, chapter 20. Do you know them?

Your Turn

1. Why do your parents have rules?
2. Why does God want us to follow His rules?

_____

_____

_____

_____

_____

Prayer

Thank You, God, for loving us enough to give us rules. You must want to protect us from sin. You are a good God! Amen.

FOLLOW THE RULES

Think of three rules that your parents and God would like you to follow. Write one rule on each of the balls below.

GOD'S AWESOME RULES

I like pleasing God.
Find out what pleases the Lord.

Ephesians 5:10

God Pleasers

"You are a people pleaser, John. You shouldn't care so much about what Ben thinks of your picture," said John's friend Mike. "Ben isn't such a great painter himself!"

"Well, I hope Mrs. Carol likes this birthday card," said John. His class was surprising their teacher with homemade birthday cards. John wanted to please Mrs. Carol. She was the best teacher he had ever had.

"I'm sure Mrs. Carol will like your card no matter what Ben says," Mike said. "When we make our teacher and our parents happy, it's like making God happy."

"You mean pleasing Mrs. Carol will please God?" asked John.

"Yes!" said Mike. "I only care if Mrs. Carol likes my card, not Ben or anyone else. I know my card will please God because I did my best."

We look for ways to please God. Do your hands know what is pleasing to God? Do your feet? Do your eyes and mouth? Learning new things in school isn't always easy. Learning what pleases God isn't easy either. One place to start is learning God's rules. They are:

1. Put God first.
2. Love God most.
3. Honor God's name.
4. Keep Sundays special.
5. Honor your father and mother.
6. Respect and protect life.
7. Be true when you marry.
8. Keep only what is yours.
9. Be honest.
10. Want only what is yours.

Obey and please God by following each one!

Your Turn

1. Why should you learn what pleases God?
2. What do these ten rules sound like?

Prayer

Dear God, help me to remember what pleases You. Make me glad and able to please You. Amen.

PLEASING GOD

Color the boy! Think of ways to please God with your hands, feet, heart, lips, eyes and ears. Write your ideas on the different body parts to help you remember.

GOD'S AWESOME RULES

God wants me to love only Him.
You shall have no other gods before me.

Exodus 20:3

Put God First

What is the most important thing to you? What is first above anything else to you?

Pretend your family had to move from your house quickly. You have a very short time to prepare to leave. You can only take a few items along to your new home. What would you take first? Would it be your cars or your action figures? What about your favorite stuffed animal? Would you leave behind the soccer prize you won?

A rich man put his money before God and Jesus. His life was very sad because he never learned to put God and Jesus first. Read about this man in the New Testament of the Bible, Luke 18:18-29.

God wants you to think of Him more often than anything or anyone. The more you know God, the easier it is to put God first. Wanting your own way isn't putting God first. Toys, TV and fun should not be more important to you than God.

Your Turn

1. What is most important to you?
2. How can you tell friends to let God be first in their life?
3. You have a very short time to prepare to leave. You can only take a few items along to your new home. Would you grab your Bible first? If not, why not?

_____

_____

_____

_____

_____

Prayer

Dear God, Don't let anything be more important to me than You. Help me to follow You each day. Amen.

GOD IS FIRST CROSSWORD

Nothing should be more important to you than God. God's first rule is to put Him first. Use the pictures below to find the words for the crossword puzzle. The words in the puzzle are things you might wrongly put before God. The answers are on page 229.

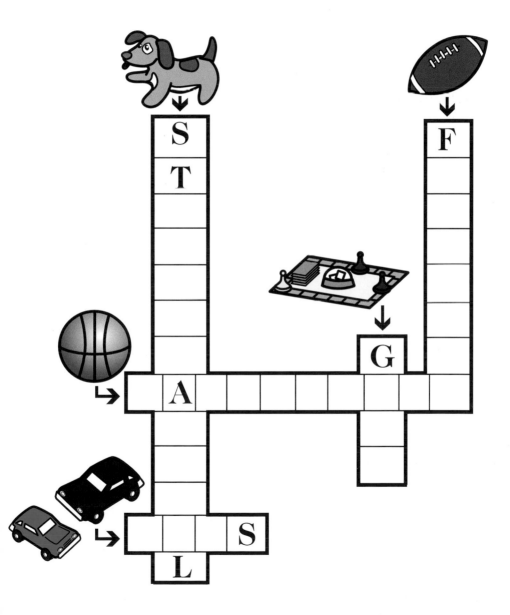

GOD'S AWESOME RULES

Keep God first in your life.
You shall not make for yourself an idol [statues to worship].
Exodus 20:4

Love God Most

"Look up here, Cliff," called Mrs. Timm. "We need to finish math before lunch."

Cliff was such a dreamer! He liked to pretend he was visiting far away places. He imagined being a sailor on a ship or a conductor on a train. He spent many hours looking out the school window.

Cliff like to play cowboys. He always wanted a pony but God had not given him one. Cliff even tried to turn Derk, his golden retriever, into a pony. He used the covers on his bed as a saddle and a leash for the reins.

No matter how hard he tried, Derk would never be a pony. God is the only one who can make ponies.

In Bible days, people made animals from gold or stone. They called these statues their gods. The people thought the idols were real. They prayed to them and worshipped them.

People can't make statues be God, just as people can't make dogs be ponies. Many people make their own gods. In other places around the world, children pray to gods who really aren't God. Whatever you love most can wrongly become your god. Your pretend gods aren't made of stone or gold. Pretend gods can be TV, sports, friends and candy. Our one true God deserves to be the one loved most. Which god do you keep first in your life?

Your Turn

1. How does God know you love Him best?
2. It is OK to like TV, sports and friends. How can these things wrongly become your god?
3. How can you keep God first in your life?

_____

_____

_____

Prayer

I am glad You are my God. Please forgive me for not always loving You more than anything else. Help me put You first in everything I say and do. Amen.

THE PONY SECRET MESSAGE

Decode the secret message on the pony's blanket about loving God first.
The answer is on page 229.

$$\frac{a}{1} \quad \frac{b}{2} \quad \frac{c}{3} \quad \frac{d}{4} \quad \frac{e}{5} \quad \frac{f}{6} \quad \frac{g}{7} \quad \frac{h}{8} \quad \frac{i}{9}$$

$$\frac{j}{10} \quad \frac{k}{11} \quad \frac{l}{12} \quad \frac{m}{13} \quad \frac{n}{14} \quad \frac{o}{15} \quad \frac{p}{16} \quad \frac{q}{17} \quad \frac{r}{18}$$

$$\frac{s}{19} \quad \frac{t}{20} \quad \frac{u}{21} \quad \frac{v}{22} \quad \frac{w}{23} \quad \frac{x}{24} \quad \frac{y}{25} \quad \frac{z}{26}$$

$$\overline{16} \; \overline{21} \; \overline{20}$$

$$\overline{7} \; \overline{15} \; \overline{4}$$

$$\overline{6} \; \overline{9} \; \overline{18} \; \overline{19} \; \overline{20}.$$

GOD'S AWESOME RULES

God is happy when I honor His name.
You shall not misuse the name of the Lord your God.
Exodus 20:7

Honor God's Name

Lazy Luke, Big Foot Don, Tricky Ricky and Dumbo Dan are examples of names misused. Has your name ever been turned into a bad or silly name? How do you feel when people use your name in a bad way?

Has your name ever been used wrongly in anger? It doesn't make you feel very good, does it?

How do you feel when your name is used in a kind way? God's name should be said in a kind way. Some people use His name and Jesus' name in a bad way. Using God's name in a bad way when you lose a game is sin. That makes God feel very sad. Using God's name for no good reason is wrong.

When and how should you use God's name? God's name should be used to tell others about Him and Jesus. God's name should be used to give thanks for all He has done. Honor and protect His name.

Can you defend His name in front of your friends? Would you wear a T-shirt with Jesus' name on it to show you love Him? Would you wear a baseball cap with the name of Jesus written on it? God is always happy when you love and honor His name in front of others.

Your Turn

1. What are some wrong ways people use God's name?
2. How can you use the name of God in good ways?

_____

_____

_____

_____

_____

Prayer

Dear God, I thank You for Your name. Your name is special to me and I love Your name. Show me how to use Your name in good ways. Amen.

THE JESUS CAP

Use a crayon to write the name "Jesus" on the baseball cap below. Color the cap to remind you to honor God's name.

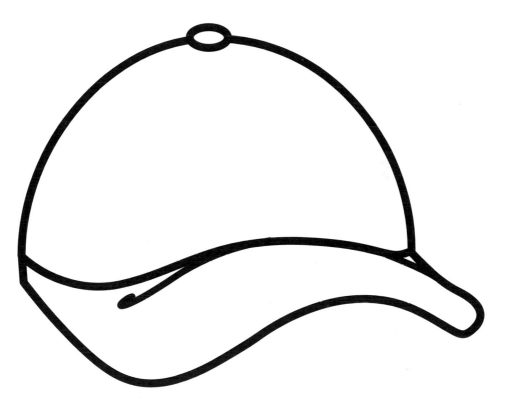

GOD'S AWESOME RULES

God wants me to make Sundays special.
Remember the Sabbath day by keeping it holy.
Exodus 20:8

Special Sundays

"Dad, why are those kids ice skating on the lake today? Shouldn't they be in Sunday school?" asked Billy as his family drove past the lake on their way to church.

"They may not know the Lord," Dad replied. "They must not know Sundays are a special day for God."

Billy thought everyone went to church on Sundays. As he listened to Dad, he wondered how he could tell those children about Jesus. He felt badly because they were missing out on God's day.

"The Bible says to remember the Sabbath," said Dad. "'Sabbath' comes from words that mean to rest from work. That is why we don't plan to do much on Sundays."

In Bible times, the Sabbath Day was a gift to God — a day of worship. Sunday is our day of worship and rest. We love and worship God at church. We should also love God and worship Him at home. Part of our worship to Him is doing good things for others, like telling friends about Jesus.

Your Turn

1. What do you do each Sunday morning and afternoon?
2. Do you think it is OK with God to miss church to play in a sports event on Sunday?
3. What would you tell someone who says he knows Jesus but doesn't go to church?

_____

_____

_____

_____

Prayer

God, help me to always keep Your day special. Teach me to use it to do something good for You and for others. Amen.

SUNDAY ICE SKATING

Matthew 12:9-13 tells that Jesus did good things for people on the Sabbath (Sunday). Write at least two things on the lake that Jesus did on the Sabbath. Write at least two things you can do on the Sabbath.

GOD'S AWESOME RULES

When I obey my parents, God is happy.
Honor your father and your mother.

Exodus 20:12

Honor Your Father and Mother

"John, you promised to empty the trash and pick up your room. Your baby sister fell over one of your cars. She could fall and get hurt," said Mom.

The Bible says, "Honor your father and mother." Honoring your parents is like promising to show them love and to obey them. It pleases God when you love and honor our parents.

How can you honor your parents? John had promised to help his mom, but he didn't keep his promise. Someone could have been hurt because John chose not to honor his parents.

John didn't know that obeying your parents makes you happy inside. If you forget to honor your parents it hurts yourself and others. What can you do to keep from making John's mistake?

Your Turn

1. Why is it good to obey your parents?
2. Name one time when you honored your parents.

_____

_____

_____

_____

_____

_____

Prayer

Dear God, forgive me for the times when I did not obey my parents. Help me to keep my promises and honor my parents. Amen.

A PROMISE NOTE

Promise God that you will try your best to honor your parents. Write a promise note to your parents about how you plan to honor and obey them.

Dear _____,

I will try my best to
___ and ___
you. I will do what
you ___ me to
do with a happy heart.

I love you!

_____
(your name)

GOD'S AWESOME RULES

My life is a gift from God.
You shall not murder.
Exodus 20:13

Respect and Protect Life

You see stories about people hurting people every day on television and radio news shows. Seeing people break God's rules makes you sad. People shouldn't hurt others.

One of God's rules says "You shall not murder." Killing a person is murder.

You might kill deer and cows for food. God isn't talking about that kind of killing in this rule. He means murder or taking the life of a person.

God wants you to know how important every human life is to Him. A baby in a mommy's tummy is important to God. Young people, middle-aged people and old people are all important to God. People who are sick are important to God. Children who can't walk and are called "handicapped" are important to God. Every living person is important to Him. Your life is a gift from God and only God can take life away. God loves all people!

Your Turn

1. Do you love people? What does God think when you hate someone? How is hate like murder?
2. How should you treat others who are mean to you?

_____

_____

_____

_____

_____

_____

Prayer

Dear God, thank You for every life. I pray that murder will stop and people will start loving each other. Teach me to love others.

RADIO RESPECT

Draw pictures on the radio of people God loves.

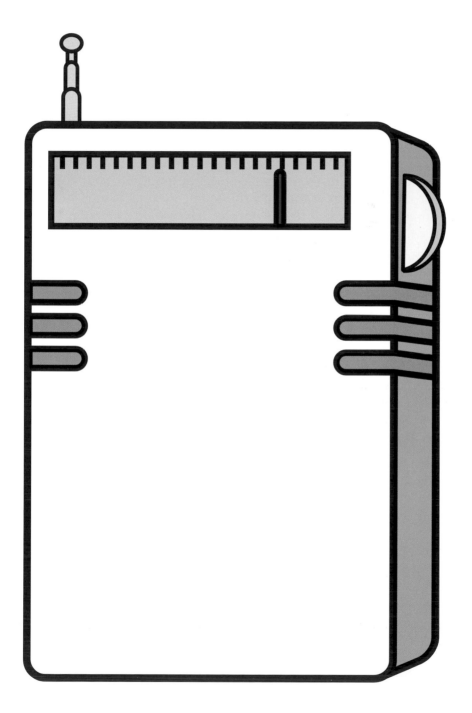

GOD'S AWESOME RULES

Teamwork is good in God's eyes.
You shall not commit adultery.
Exodus 20:14

When You Marry, Be True

"Let Ryan be our team captain," said the guys on the basketball team. Ryan said he wanted to be the leader. He told each guy on the team where they would play.

Scott said, "I quit if I have to play forward. I want to play guard, not forward."

Another boy quit Ryan's team to join another team because he couldn't play where he wanted on the team. No one wanted to be true to the team unless they had their own way. They wanted to be on the team, but they wanted to play by their own rules.

The boys on Ryan's team weren't committed or faithful to the team. Committing to something means not quitting when things don't go your way. Husbands and wives are like teams. God wants husbands and wives to stay on the same team. A husband and wife team should be committed to each other.

When you get married, it is good to pick the right team player. If you pick the right one then you will be on a team that stays together. The Bible says, "You shall not commit adultery." Leaving a husband or wife for another person is adultery. God wants married people to love Him and stay on the same team.

Your Turn

1. Do you or your friends have parents who are not on the same team anymore? Can you pray for them?
2. Why is this rule important?
3. What does it mean to be faithful to someone?

Prayer

Please help me to be on the same team with my friends and family. Help me to pick friends that love You and are faithful to You. I pray husbands and wives in our world would stay on the same team. Amen.

TEAM PLAYING

Draw a picture of yourself on the team to remind you that God wants husbands and wives to stay on the same team.

GOD'S AWESOME RULES

God is happy when we are honest.
You shall not steal.

Exodus 20:15

Keep Only What Is Yours

Steve and his father were shopping for family Christmas gifts. In the Christmas aisle Steve spotted an awesome tree decoration. It was his favorite action figure made to hang on a Christmas tree.

This would look great on our tree, he thought.

"Can I buy it?" Steve asked his dad.

"No, son, we have enough tree decorations," replied Dad.

Steve begged his dad to buy it for him, but Dad kept saying no. Steve couldn't take his eyes off of the action figure. He really wanted it! As Steve and his father headed for the checkout, Steve asked if he could go to the bathroom. "OK," said Dad, "but meet me at the front of the store."

Steve wandered back to the Christmas aisle. He looked up and down the aisle to be sure no one was watching. Then he slipped the decoration into his pocket.

Won't Steve's dad find the decoration when Steve tries to place it on the tree? He will find out that Steve was stealing. God's Word says that stealing is wrong. God knows when you do wrong.

Remember: God loves you. God forgives you when you say you are sorry and mean it. Saying you're sorry and asking God to forgive you is like washing your hands. It makes you feel clean and look clean in God's eyes.

You can also keep your hands clean for God by not stealing. There was a man in the Bible who used his hands to take money from people. Once he met Jesus, he saw that stealing was wrong. He was sorry and God forgave him. Read about it in Luke 19:1-10.

Your Turn

1. What do you think Steve's dad did when he found the decoration?
2. Why was it wrong for Steve to steal even a small decoration?

Prayer

Dear God, I thank You that when I do wrong, You still love me. Teach me not to steal. Amen.

BAR OF SOAP

One way to keep your hands clean is by not stealing. Write the Bible verse about stealing on the bar of soap.

GOD'S AWESOME RULES

God wants me to say kind things about others.
You shall not give a false testimony against your neighbor.
Exodus 20:16

Be Honest

Two boys laughed as the teacher called on Jay to read aloud in class. Jay was a very smart boy, but he had a problem reading aloud. It was hard for him. "Boy, is he dumb," said one of the boys.

The other boy listened and joked too. He even added something to the false talk about Jay.

Have you heard people make fun of someone like these boys made fun of Jay? Jay would feel bad if he knew those boys talked about him. The two boys said false things about him.

One of God's rules says, "You shall not give a false testimony against your neighbor." That is what the two boys were doing. They were giving a false testimony against Jay.

Lying makes your mouth like a trap. When you speak lies about someone the mouth traps you into sin. The mouth traps the other person too. The lie may trap that person into believing there is something wrong with him.

Saying things that aren't true about people is lying and it is sin. Talking badly about other people doesn't please God.

Your Turn

1. What would you say to the boys talking about Jay?
2. What does God think about lying to parents and friends?
3. Is it all right to tell a small lie to someone? What about a small lie about someone?

Prayer

Help me to never give a false testimony about someone. Keep me from hurting others with lying words. Amen.

MOUTH TRAPS

Do not let your mouth be a trap for sin. On the mouth trap, write the Bible verse for this lesson and color the trap.

GOD'S AWESOME RULES

I can be happy with what I have.
You shall not covet...your neighbor's house.

Exodus 20:17

Want Only What's Yours

Nelson could stand at the monkey cage all day. Monkeys were Nelson's favorite animals at the zoo.

He often watched the monkeys eat dinner. Food was slipped onto the cage floor right in front of the monkeys. One of the monkeys would grab the food as it entered the cage then quickly climb the tree.

Nelson watched as the monkey put a banana into her mouth and placed an apple under her arm. Next, a head of lettuce and fresh mangoes were rolled onto the cage floor. The monkey climbed down the tree and picked up the mangoes.

Was she afraid the other monkeys would get part of her food? The monkey was selfish. When she saw the lettuce, she put down the mangoes and picked up the lettuce. Then she climbed down the tree, grabbed the mangoes and ran up the tree again. So much food had been stuffed into her mouth at one time that she couldn't enjoy eating it. The monkey wanted more and more.

The rule "You shall not covet" means not to want more and more. Be happy with what God gives and how much He gives. Wanting more and more will only make you unhappy. The monkey couldn't enjoy the food because she had too much. What about you? If you want something and are willing to hurt someone to get it, stop. Pray and ask God if you really need it.

Your Turn

1. What can you do when you feel you want what you don't have?
2. When is wanting something you don't have OK?

Prayer

Dear God, help me not to want everything I see in ads on TV. Teach me not to want everything like the monkey did. Show me how to love You and be happy with what I have. Amen.

HAPPINESS CAGE

There are two monkey cages. One cage shows a monkey who doesn't want everything it sees. The other cage shows a monkey who wants all the food that comes into the cage. He keeps it for himself. Which monkey would God say is the happiest? Put a smile on the face of the monkey who is obeying. Put a sad face on monkey who wants it all.

GOD'S AWESOME RULES

I want to love God with all of my heart.
Love the Lord our God with all your heart and with
all your soul and with all your mind.

Matthew 22:37-38

My Heart Is God's

It is fun to build with wooden blocks. To build a tower you must find the right size and shape of blocks to stack. You must find blocks that fit together so the tower will stand without falling over.

In a similar way, the pieces of a puzzle are locked together to make a picture. Each piece is important for the puzzle to look like a picture.

God put all 10 of His rules together for you to keep in your heart. Each rule is important for you to learn. God's rules can protect you from life's storms and keep you safe.

As you learn to keep God's rules you become more like Jesus. Keeping the 10 rules in your heart is like putting something together that is good.

There is one last piece for the rule puzzle to be complete. It is the greatest rule God gives. "Love the Lord our God with all your heart..." (Matthew 22:37-38). That piece makes the puzzle complete!

Your Turn

1. How can this rule help you with the other rules?
2. What does it mean to love God with your heart?

_____

_____

_____

_____

_____

_____

Prayer

Lord, thank You for all Your rules and Your great love for me. Amen.

PUZZLE BLOCKS

Can you remember God's rules? Fill in the missing words on the puzzle blocks below. The answer is on page 230.

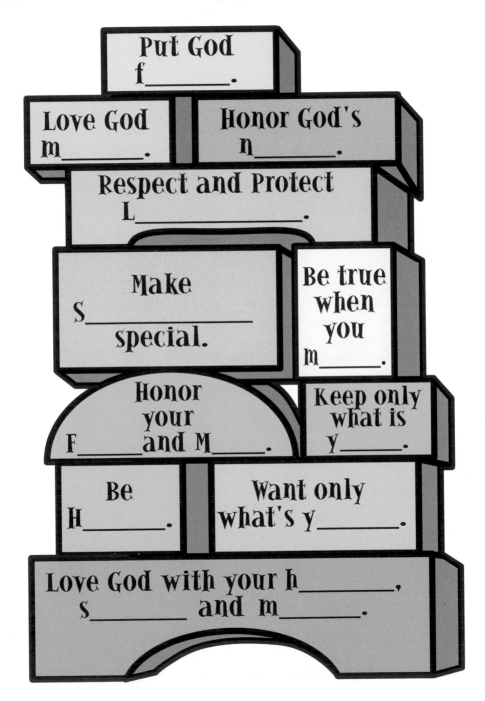

Put God
f_____.

Love God
m_____.

Honor God's
n_____.

Respect and Protect
L_____.

Make
S_____
special.

Be true
when
you
m____.

Honor
your
F_____ and M____.

Keep only
what is
y_____.

Be
H_____.

Want only
what's y_____.

Love God with your h_____,
S_____ and m_____.

GOD'S AWESOME RULES

I want to please God in every way.
Live a life worthy of the Lord that may please him in every way.
Colossians 1:10

Learning to Please

"Vacation is finally here," said Jeff. "No school for two weeks!"

"You won't stop learning because school is out," said Dad.

"What can I learn at home?" asked Jeff.

"I know a lesson that is easy to learn," said Dad. Dad grabbed his Bible from the top of the desk. He turned to the New Testament.

"Here it is!" said Dad. " 'Live a life worthy of the Lord that may please him in every way.' Colossians 1:10."

"Is that the lesson?" asked Jeff?

"Yes!" answered Dad. "Learning to please God is a good lesson."

"I understand!" said Jeff. "You should find out what pleases God. But how do I find out what pleases God?"

"A good place to begin is by reading the Bible just like this," said Dad. "Choosing to obey your mom and me will help. Putting your friends first and helping them pleases God. Obeying God's ten rules will also help. Is the lesson hard so far?"

"I already try to do those things," said Jeff.

"That's great!" replied Dad. "Do your mouth, hands and feet always seek to please God? Do you want to please God more than yourself?"

"I understand what you mean, Dad. I guess I still have a few more things to learn about pleasing God," said Jeff.

"That's my guy!" said Dad as he put his arm around Jeff. "Don't worry, your mom and I will help you."

Your Turn

1. Why is it hard to please God?
2. Name some ways to please God with your mouth, hands and feet.

_____

_____

_____

Prayer

God, help me to please You. Help me to always want to please You and my parents. Help me to please You and to help my friends. Amen.

GOD PLEASER PUZZLE

Solve the puzzle below. Think of ways to please God with your mouth, feet and hands. Follow the arrows by the pictures and fill in the missing letters. The answer is on page 230.

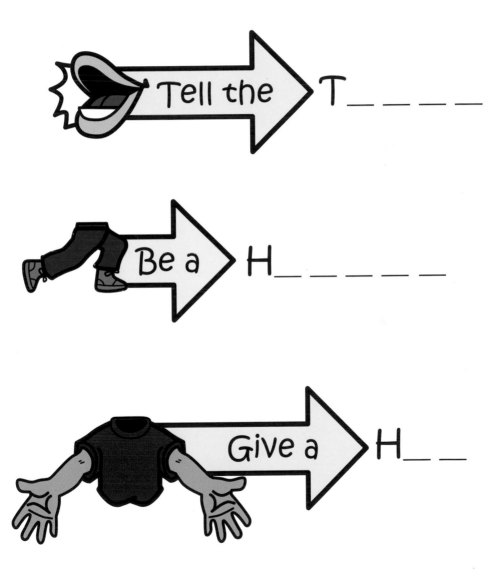

Tell the T _ _ _ _

Be a H _ _ _ _ _

Give a H _ _

GOTTA KNOW ABOUT ME

GOTTA KNOW ABOUT ME

I can give joy to others.
Laughter is good medicine.
Proverbs 17:22

Knock, Knock Jokes

"Mom, Dale has been sad since his dad moved out," said Greg.

"His parents' parting has been hard on him," said Mom.

"But, I made him smile today," said Greg.

"Oh! How did you do that?" asked Mom.

"I told him a knock-knock joke. It really cheered him up," said Greg.

"Great!" said Mom. "Jokes are good for cheering someone. That reminds me of a Bible verse: 'A cheerful heart is good medicine.' "

"Does that mean that my knock-knock jokes can heal?" asked Greg.

"Yes!" said Mom. "It also means that God wants us to laugh and have fun."

"God must like laughter," said Greg.

"It's OK to be sad over problems. But I hope Dale can be happy even through his sadness," said Mom.

Only God can fill our hearts with great joy. Jesus loved us so much that He died on the cross for our sins. He died for the sad things that happen. That is the kind of love that can make Greg happy, and it will make you happy too.

Your Turn

1. Why wasn't Dale happy inside? Do you think he knew God wanted to help him?
2. How do you know God loves you?
3. How do you feel inside when you know God loves you?

_____

_____

_____

_____

_____

Prayer

Dear God, You have put gladness in my heart. Help me to know Your love for me so I can be happy inside. Amen.

JOKES FOR GOD

Make up a knock-knock joke that cheers someone up and tells them about God at the same time. (Example: Knock, Knock. Who's there? God so. God so who? God so loved the world and you!)

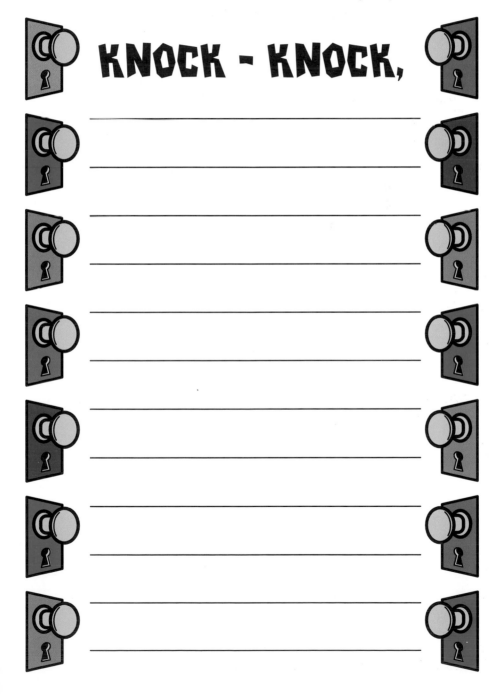

KNOCK - KNOCK,

GOTTA KNOW ABOUT ME

I learn more about Jesus each day.
*Crave pure milk, so that by it you
may grow up in your salvation.*

1 Peter 2:2

Big for Jesus

"Can I go with you to Jake's house?" Don wanted to follow his older brother everywhere.

"No," his brother said. "You're too little."

"Can I go to the movies with you?" Don asked.

"No, you're too little," said his brother.

"Can I go to the baseball game with you?"

"No, you're too little."

Don's brother would repeat the same answer again and again.

When will I ever grow up and do something fun? thought Don.

Some day Don will grow up and so will you. You may be too little to do some things now. But you are never too little to learn about Jesus and His love for you.

The Bible says you can always learn more about Jesus. That's called "getting big" for Jesus. Peter, Jesus's friend, said we should grow big in our love for Jesus.

When you believe God, you begin to grow big in God. Don wanted to grow up so he could follow his big brother. You can be big in knowing Jesus now! Read your Bible, pray and tell others about Jesus. Then you will grow big in Jesus. How big are you?

Your Turn

1. What are some ways you learn about Jesus?
2. How can your love for God keep growing?

_____

_____

_____

_____

Prayer

Dear God, I want to keep growing as a follower of Jesus. Please help me to grow. Lead me and teach me more about Jesus so I can be big in Him. Amen.

JESUS SCALE

Standing on a scale tells you how much your body weighs. But you can be big in knowing Jesus now! How big are you in knowing Jesus? If you are small that's OK. You will grow in Jesus as you pray and read your Bible. Write an S (small), M (medium) or L (large) on the scale. Then circle where you want to be.

GOTTA KNOW ABOUT ME

> God will not forget me.
> *I will not forget you!*
> Isaiah 49:15

God Won't Forget

It was dark as the Stamps set out to drive to Grandma's farm. The rain fell hard on the windshield. Dad couldn't see the road in front of him. Pretty soon the rain fell heavy. Dad realized they were on the wrong road.

"It's raining so hard I missed my turn," said Dad. "Now we're lost."

The Stamps' two boys, Joe and Brian, began to cry.

"Are we really lost, Daddy? We'll never get to Grandma's now!"

Dad pulled over to the side of the road.

"Let's just sit here and wait for the storm to die down," said Dad. " We will get to Grandma's house. Besides, God knows where we are. If we pray, He will help us find our way."

"Can I pray, Daddy?" asked Brian.

"Sure," said Dad.

"Dear God, please help us find our way to Grandma's," Brian prayed.

Soon Dad saw flashing lights in the rear view mirror of the car.

"It's the highway patrol," said Dad. The patrolman led them back to the main road.

"See, kids, as the Bible says, 'The Lord is good. He cares for those who trust Him.' God kept us safe and sound," said Dad.

The Stamps made it to Grandma's in time for a bedtime snack. Dad trusted that God would never forget them.

Don't be afraid to ask God for help. You are very special to Him. God won't forget you! Just trust in Him.

Your Turn

1. Were you ever lost? Were you afraid?
2. What does God do when you trust Him?

_____

_____

Prayer

Dear God, I should trust You at all times. Forgive me for forgetting You even though You don't forget me. Help me to trust that You won't forget me. Amen.

POLICE SCRAMBLE

Find the words in the Bible verse that are on the raindrops. Put them in the right order on the lines below the highway police car. The answer is on page 230.

$$\overline{}_1 \quad \overline{}_2\overline{}_3\overline{}_4\overline{}_5 \quad \overline{}_6\overline{}_7\overline{}_8$$

$$\overline{}_9\overline{}_{10}\overline{}_{11}\overline{}_{12}\overline{}_{13}\overline{}_{14} \quad \overline{}_{15}\overline{}_{16}\overline{}_{17}!$$

GOTTA KNOW ABOUT ME

I can keep my eyes on Jesus.
Let us fix our eyes on Jesus.

Hebrews 12:2

Eyes for Jesus

Look around! You see many things each day. Your eyes see television, video games and sports games.

Seeing those things isn't bad. But Jesus wants you to think about Him more than those things.

A boy named Nick didn't have his eyes on Jesus. His eyes were on himself.

"Nick, Mrs. Rose needs someone to watch Buffy, her cat," said Mom. "When?" asked Nick.

"For the next two days," said mom.

"Why?" he asked.

"She is going into the hospital for surgery," said Mom.

"Oh, do I have to?" asked Nick. "Ben and I are going to play basketball after school. I don't have time to help."

"You should help Mrs. Rose. You can play basketball with Ben any day," said Mom. "Keeping an eye on her cat is keeping your eyes on Jesus. Helping Mrs. Rose is like helping Jesus."

"When our eyes are on Jesus," said Mom, "we want to help others. Jesus helped others so we should too."

Nick learned to think more about Jesus than himself. That is fixing your eyes on Jesus.

Your Turn

1. Is there someone you know who God wants you to help?
2. How do you feel when your eyes are on Jesus?

Prayer

God, help me to be ready to help others. Show me people who I can help. Show me when my eyes aren't on You. Amen.

SEE YOUR VERSE

Keep your eyes on Jesus by knowing His word. Follow the directions below.

Learn the verse

Let us fix our eyes on Jesus. Hebrews 12:2

Know the verse

Do the word dot-to-dot using the words of the verse.

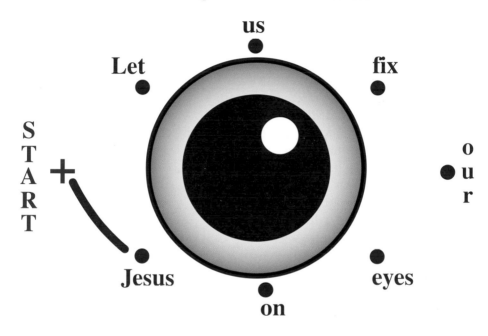

Write the verse

Write the verse on the lines below.

_____

_____

_____

_____

Think about this

Learn to fix your eyes on Jesus. Read the Bible and obey His words.
Do you know Jesus as your Lord and Savior?

GOTTA KNOW ABOUT ME

God helps me do many things.
I can do everything through Him who gives me strength.
Philippians 4:13

Being Strong

Mike loved watching his father lift weights. He could lift a 200-pound weight over his head!

My dad is the strongest man in the world, thought Mike.

"How strong are you, Daddy?" Mike asked.

"I'm not that strong, bud." said Dad.

"Will you show me how to lift weights, Dad?" asked Mike.

"These weights are too heavy for you, Mike. But I'll help you lift one! We'll do it together," Dad said.

"After we lift weights will you help me with my math paper?" asked Mike.

"Sure! We can do math together too," said Dad.

He told Mike to put his hands on the weight bar. Dad stood behind Mike placing his hands over Mike's. Dad's big hands covered Mike's so together they could move the weights.

God probably won't help you lift weights. But He will help you do good things for Him. The Bible says we can do all things with the help of Jesus. Jesus will help you do what is good for you. With His help, you can be strong even when you feel weak. All you need to do is ask Jesus for help, and He is there.

Your Turn

1. Why couldn't Mike move the weights by himself?
2. What are some things with which you need help?
3. Why does Jesus want to help you?

Prayer

Dear Jesus, I know that with Your help I can do anything. With Your help, I can be what You want me to be. With Your help I can do good things for You. Amen.

GOD'S HANDS

Let God be strong for you. Under Jesus' hand, write something with which you need His help.

GOTTA KNOW ABOUT ME

I was wonderfully made by God.

I praise You because I am fearfully and wonderfully made.

Psalm 139:14

God Made Me

Collin loved looking at his baby pictures.

"Look, Mom," said Collin. He held up his first baby picture. "See my nose, Mom? It was so small!"

"You're just as wonderful today as you were then," Mom said. "Babies are such miracles."

She picked up the photo. "Collin, just look at your little feet, ears and fingers in this picture. You are different from anyone else. See the little mole on your right ear?" she asked.

"See! It's still there," pointed Collin. "I think that mole was a mistake."

"No!" frowned Mom. "God doesn't make mistakes. He put that mole there. It is part of who you are. I can't think of anything so wonderfully made as our bodies.

"God has something special planned for your life, Collin. Be happy with who you are. You're perfect because God made you."

Your Turn

1. Who made you? Why?
2. What wonderful things can your hands and feet do?
3. God made you! Then to whom do you belong?

_____

_____

_____

_____

_____

Prayer

Thank You, God, for me. I am wonderfully made so I can serve You, God. Help me to take care of my body. Don't let me compare myself with others. Show me Your plan for my life. Amen.

EAR PUZZLE

Decode the secret message on the ear. Use the hearts to help you decode the message. The answer is on page 230.

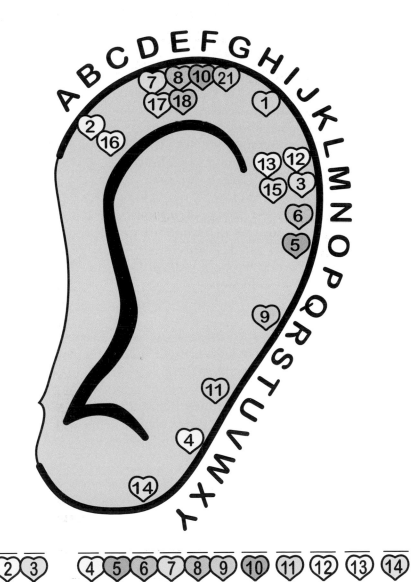

GOTTA KNOW ABOUT ME

I will pray for friends who hurt me.
Bless those who curse you, pray for those who mistreat you.
Luke 6:28

Prayers for Friends

"I won't play with those boys anymore," cried Roy. "I'm always picked last when we play teams. They are so mean to me."

"What did they do this time?" asked Mom.

"They called me names. Billy Banks hit me in the face with a soccer ball." Mom listened carefully to Roy. His story reminded her of her own childhood. A mean girl named Liz would hide her school lunch. Other girls made fun of the clothes she wore to school.

"It's easy to feel hatred toward mean kids," she said. "Roy, I know how you feel. The Bible says, 'Do good to those who hate you.' God wants us to love even mean kids. He also wants us to forgive them."

"That's too hard," said Roy. "I just want to punch them in the stomach." "What could we do for those boys, Roy? Let's invite them to your birthday party," said Mom.

"I know!" said Roy. "I can offer to keep score for them in the next neighborhood game."

"Let's pray right now for those boys," said Mom.

Roy prayed for the boys each night before he went to bed. He found ways to be nice to the mean boys. It took a while, but God answered Roy's prayers. He became friends with some of the boys on his block. Roy even invited them to church. Once they heard about Jesus, they felt badly for how they had treated Roy. Roy did the right thing.

Your Turn

1. How do mean kids make you feel?
2. Do you feel good when you get back at someone who has been mean to you? What would Jesus say?

Prayer

Dear Jesus, please help me love mean girls and boys. Help me not to be upset when mean kids hurt me. Remind me to pray for them every day. Amen.

SOCCER BALL PRAYER

Use the soccer ball below as a prayer journal! Begin praying for friends who hurt you. Also pray for kids who are mean.

GOTTA KNOW ABOUT ME

I don't want to miss God's best.
Yet not as I will, but as You will.

Matthew 26:39

God's Best for Me

Sometimes parents tell you to do things you don't understand. They tell you to wash behind your ears, or not to forget to put on your bike helmet. "Eat everything on your dinner plate," they probably say.

Parents ask you to do things you might not like. Did you know they have good reasons for telling you what to do? If you love your parents, you will trust them to do what's best for you.

It's the same way with God. If you love God, you can trust Him to do what's best for you. Loving God is saying, "Not what I want God, but what You want."

God always wants the best for you. It's God's love that makes Him want the best for you. God doesn't want anything or anyone to hurt you. Can you help God do what's best for you and others? Obeying your parents helps God do what's best for you.

Your Turn

1. Why should you let God decide what is best?
2. Why do you miss God's best for you?
3. How can you find out God's best for you?

_____

_____

_____

_____

_____

_____

Prayer

Dear God, You know what's best for me. Help me to love Your best for me. When my parents tell me to do something, remind me that they are acting for You, and You know what's best for me. Amen.

GOD'S-BEST BIKE HELMET

Next to the bicycle helmet with the happy face, write three things that are God's best to do (example: wear a coat when it's cold). Next to the bicycle helmet with the sad face, write three things that aren't God's best to do (example: watch a movie with bad words).

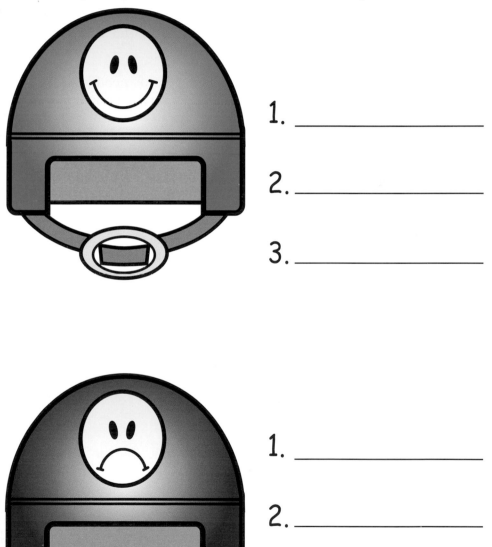

1. _____

2. _____

3. _____

1. _____

2. _____

3. _____

GOTTA KNOW ABOUT ME

I want to be a child of God.
Those who believe in His name, He gave
the right to become children of God.

John 1:12

God's Child

Grant's brother had to have 10 stitches put in his head because they had gotten into a fight and Grant hit him with a tennis racket.

One day at school Grant's teacher sent him to the principal. He had thrown spit balls on the walls. Grant told his parents and teachers he didn't have to obey them.

The children's pastor at Grant's church talked with him. The pastor asked Grant, "Do you believe Jesus died for you? Do you know He loves you?"

"Of course, I'm a Christian. I go to church, don't I? My parents are Christians, aren't they?" said Grant.

"But going to church doesn't make you a child of God," said the pastor. "Every person must decide whether or not to follow Jesus. Your parents can't make that decision for you. No one can, except you."

"A child of God loves Jesus and wants to follow Him," the pastor said. "A child of God likes what Jesus likes. He wants to please God and obey Him."

The pastor was trying to tell Grant that loving Jesus is doing things His way. Then you can become a child of God.

Grant told his pastor, "I'm sorry for the trouble I have caused everyone. I don't want to do things my way anymore."

"Let's pray together," said the pastor.

Your Turn

1. Grant thought he was a child of God because he went to church and his parents knew Jesus. Was he right or wrong? Why?
2. How do you become a child of God?'
3. How do you show others you are a child of God?

Prayer

Dear God, I want to be Your child. I don't want to do things my way anymore. I want to do things Your way, God. Amen.

GOD'S CHILD PUZZLE

Grant wanted to be a child of God. Fill in the missing letters below. Find out what He needed to do to become a child of God. The answer is on page 230.

Th_s_ wh_ b_lie_e
i_ Hi_ _ame,
He gave t_ _
r_ght t_
be_ o_e
chi_dre_
_f ____.
John 1:12

GOTTA KNOW ABOUT ME

God wants my heart to be clean.
Wash me and I will be whiter than snow.

Psalm 51:7

Clean-Up Time

"Brent, it's clean-up time. You and I need to clean the tool shed," said Dad.

"Be sure to change that white T-shirt before you start cleaning," said Mom.

"Oh, this old thing. I don't care if it gets dirty," said Brent as he pointed to a spot. "See? It already has a jelly stain on it."

"Put that T-shirt into the washing machine, Brent. Maybe I can fight that stain with bleach," said Mom. "I can tell it's going to be hard to keep your T-shirts clean. Thank God for bleach."

A dirty T-shirt like Brent's can always be cleaned. Bleach can wash away dirt and stains. But it can't wash away the bad things you say and do. It can't wash a person's sins away. Only God can do that.

When God forgives your wrong-doings, they are bleached away. God doesn't care if your T-shirt is clean. He does care if you are clean in your mind and heart.

Would you like a clean heart? Then be sorry for doing wrong. Ask God to forgive you for doing things your way and not His way. God will forgive you and make you clean again!

Your Turn

1. Could Brent's mom wash his heart for him?
2. Who can wash Brent's heart and your heart?
3. How many sins can God wash? Are there any sins that can't be washed away?

_____

_____

_____

_____

_____

Prayer

Dear God, forgive me of my sins (name some of your recent sins). I want to be made clean again. Amen.

CLEAN-UP MAZE

Clean up your heart! Color white each of Brent's dirty T-shirts that show sin as they lead to a clean heart and mind. Only Jesus can wash your heart clean.

GOTTA KNOW ABOUT ME

I want to be ready for Jesus.
You must also be ready, because the son of man will come.

Luke 12:40

Looking for Jesus

A boy lived on a farm with his parents and sisters. One day his father told them some bad news. He said he would need to go away for a while.

"Our farm will be taken away if I don't get work in the city," said the father.

The boy was very sad at first. Then the father said, "I will return when I have money to save the farm. I love you all and I'll think about you while I'm gone."

The boy, his sisters and his mother worked very hard while the father was gone. They milked cows, fed chickens and cleaned the barn. Life was hard and there were problems while he was gone. But they were happy because they knew the father would return.

That's the way it is with Jesus. Living here on earth is sometimes hard work. We may have problems and sadness. But Jesus has promised He will return to earth someday. He loves us and wants us to be with Him in heaven. God doesn't want us to worry. We don't need to be afraid of Jesus coming again. We can be happy and cheerful now. We are loved by God and we'll be safe when Jesus comes again. Get ready for Jesus to come again by loving others and working hard for Jesus.

Your Turn

1. How can you be ready for Jesus to return?
2. What keeps you from being ready for Jesus' return?

_____

_____

_____

_____

_____

Prayer

God, help me to be ready for Jesus to come again. Help me to love You and serve You while I wait for you. Amen.

THE WAITING BARN

The boy worked hard to care for the farm while waiting for his father to return. Get ready for Jesus' coming by working hard for Him. What can you do for Jesus before He returns? Write inside the barn the things you can do.

GOTTA KNOW ABOUT ME

God wants me to love others.
Let us love one another.

1 John 4:7

A Change of Heart

Andy wanted to love Jesus by being nice to others. But there was one boy he couldn't be nice to: Jeff Burns! Jeff had made fun of Andy just because Andy was left-handed. Jeff called Andy "lefty" and other names in front of the other kids.

"Aren't you using the wrong hand? What's wrong with your right hand?" he would ask Andy.

Andy's feelings were hurt. He couldn't forget it. Andy wouldn't talk to Jeff or look at him. He hated him.

Then one week in children's church, Andy heard the teacher talk about love. She read from the Bible, "Beloved, let us love one another." She said that loving others shows Jesus you love Him.

The teacher also told how God sent Jesus to die and pay for our sins. Andy began to think about Jeff. He thought, *If Jesus loves me, I should love others. If I don't love Jeff, I will make Jesus sad.*

Andy's heart changed. Andy knew he couldn't say he loved Jesus, and keep hating Jeff.

I want to always love Jesus and others, he thought. At that moment, Andy asked God to forgive him for hating Jeff. The next time he saw Jeff, he said, "Hi." He was always friendly after that day in children's church. Jeff didn't change, but Andy did. That made Andy feel closer to Jesus.

Your Turn

1. How does hating someone make you feel?
2. If you want to love Jesus, how will you treat others?

_____

_____

_____

Prayer

Dear God, thank You for being so willing to forgive me. I love You and Jesus. I want to be a blessing to Jesus. Teach me to always love others. Amen.

THE LEFT HAND

Trace the dots to make a left hand on this page. The solution is on page 230. Think of three people who have hurt your feelings. Write their names on the lines in the left hand below. Pray for them and ask God to help you love them.

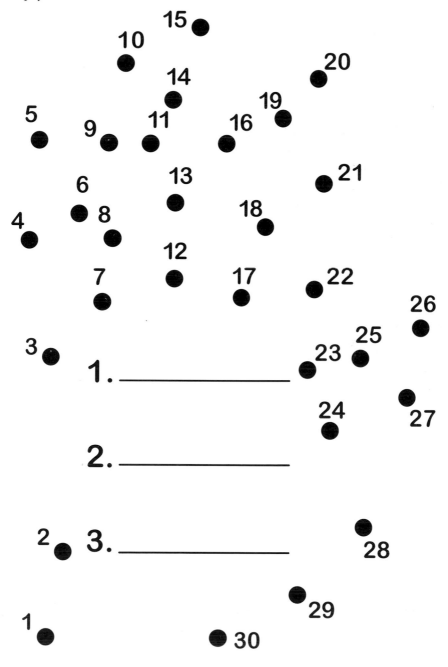

GOTTA KNOW ABOUT ME

I won't get tired of doing right.
And for you, my brother, never tire of doing right.

2 Thessalonians 3:13

The Right Circle

The first time Dave played Twister™ with his sister, he lost. With every turn, Dave's arms and legs twisted around hers. Pretty soon he lost his balance. Dave fell flat on the mat.

Do you sometimes feel like Dave and that game? If you don't go the right way, you can end up doing wrong things.

Preston went to a store. He wished he had enough money to buy some candy. But he had no money. When he went into the store, the clerk was on the phone. Preston could have stolen the candy if he wanted.

It was like Preston was on one of those colored circles and ready to move. If he moved one way, and walked out of the store, he would please God. If he moved a different way and stole the candy, he would do wrong. God wouldn't be pleased and he would get caught. Preston didn't take the candy. He kept his balance!

Your Turn

1. Why was it important for Dave to stay on the right circle?
2. Where does sin take you?
3. How does the Bible help you go the right way?

_____

_____

_____

_____

_____

_____

Prayer

Dear God, help me understand how to do right. Make me willing to follow the directions in the Bible. When I do wrong, put me back on the right circle. Amen.

THE TWISTER™ GAME

As long as David stayed on the right circle he was okay. Moving his arms and legs to the wrong circle made him fall down. Look at the twister mat below. Color the circles that tell the right thing to do. The answer is on page 231.

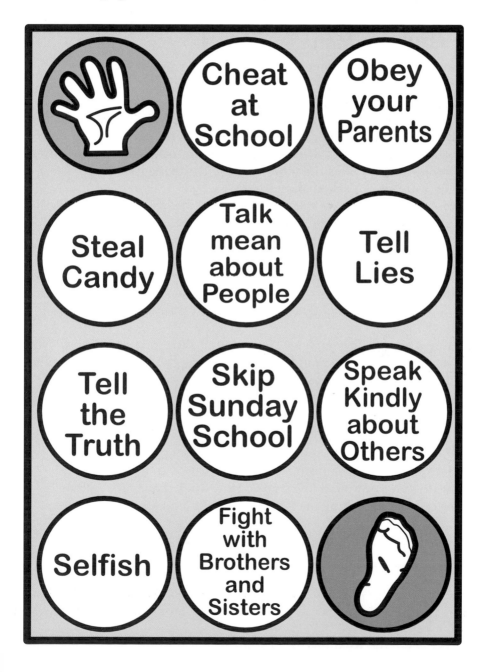

GOTTA KNOW ABOUT ME

Knowing God makes me smile.
If one of you is happy, he should sing praises.

James 15:13

The Grumpy Man

Tim slid into his parents' van after school.

"Hi, buddy!" said Mom. "How was your day?"

"Not so hot!" answered Tim.

Mom turned her face toward him and asked, "Why the long face, son?" Tim glanced at Mom. "Well," he said, "grumpy Mr. Martin, the lunch room aid, got mad at me today. I didn't even do anything! He made Tony and me clean off lunch tables. He said we were throwing food."

"Well were you?" asked Mom.

"No," assured Tim. "It was Jason McFee! We weren't doing anything. We were just eating our lunches."

"Sometimes adults like Mr. Martin make mistakes," Mom said. "Maybe you had better stay out of his way."

"Do you think Mr. Martin is a happy person?" asked Tim.

"He doesn't look happy," Mom said as she started the car and smiled at Tim. "You can tell when people are happy on the inside."

"How?" asked Tim.

"They smile on the outside," said Mom. "But, only God knows what's in his heart. The Bible says in Psalm 4:7 that God filled David's heart with joy. David knew God! That's what made him happy inside and out."

Tim thought for a minute. "Maybe Mr. Martin doesn't know God and His love," he said. "I'm going to pray for him that he will."

Your Turn

1. What makes you grumpy?
2. How do you know God loves you? How does that make you feel?
3. How does being happy on the inside make you smile on the outside?

Prayer

Dear God, help me to know You. I want to know Your love for me. Amen.

HAPPY FACES

Draw a happy face on the lines under the pictures showing the boys who are happy. Draw a sad face on the lines under the pictures showing boys who are sad. The answer is on page 231.

HAPPY FACE

SAD FACE

GOTTA KNOW ABOUT ME

I can be great for God.
*Whoever wants to become great among
you must be your servant.*

Matthew 20:26

The Greatest

Nathan Phillips had saved every one of his favorite basketball player's trading cards. He plopped down in his bean bag chair to watch Jordan play his final basketball game. The star was about to leave basketball forever.

When the game was over, a special award awaited him. The award was to honor him and his many years of playing great basketball. The player stepped up to the speaker and accepted the award.

The aged basketball star spoke to the people. A tear ran down his cheek as he said, "I thank God for letting me play a game I love so much. I want to give the rest of my life to serving God. I will use my talents to help God. The award I carry in my hand is for God."

Other men on his team wanted to be great like him. They wanted to be great so people would know them. Their eyes were on themselves. But this great player didn't want to be great for others. He wanted to be great for God. His eyes were on God and not on himself.

Your Turn

1. How does a person get to be great?
2. People try to be great without God. Can you really be great without God?

_____

_____

_____

_____

_____

_____

Prayer

Dear God, I'm glad I know You. Help me keep my eyes on You. Let me be great for You and not people. Amen.

GREATNESS HOOP

Beside each ball, write a way you can be great for God at home, school and church.

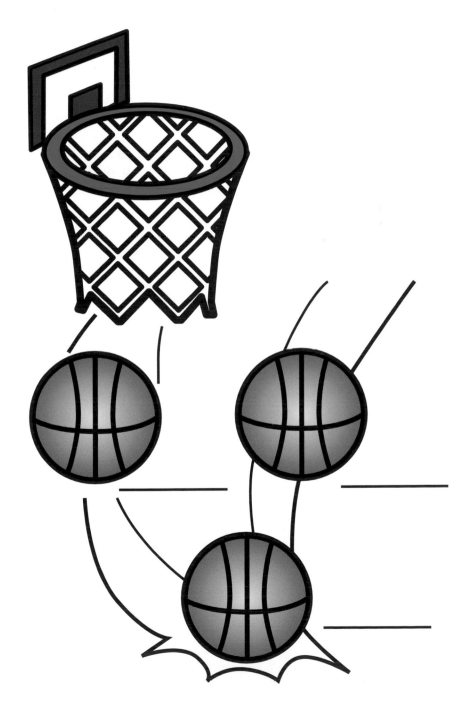

GOTTA KNOW ABOUT ME

God wants me to change my world.
You are the light of the world.

Matthew 5:14

I'm A World Changer

Joey spun the globe on the desk in his bedroom.

The world seems like a very big place. I sure hope my cousins are safe, he thought.

Joey's uncle, aunt and cousins are missionaries in a far away place. War has broken out there. They had to escape from that place and go somewhere else. They got away just before the bombs fell.

"What are you doing Joe?" asked Mom.

"I'm thinking about my cousins," Joe said.

"I know what you mean," said mom. "I have been thinking about them too. They have been put in danger in order to tell others about Jesus."

Joey plopped down on his bed. "How can God change such a big world?" he asked.

"Nothing is impossible with God, Joe," said Mom. "Everyone who knows Jesus and loves Him can make a difference in the world."

"Do you mean that I don't have to go to a far away place to make a difference for Jesus?" asked Joe.

"That's right," answered Mom. "You can be a world changer at school, in the neighborhood and on your baseball team. A world changer is a light in a dark world. You can be a world changer by just loving your family."

"I guess you're right, Mom. I never thought of that before," said Joe. "I know I should be nicer to my brother."

"That's a great start," laughed Mom. "And while you're thinking about being a world changer, please clean your room."

Your Turn

1. Would you like to be a missionary? Where?
2. How can prayer change the world around you?

Prayer

Dear God, thank You for loving me so I can be a world changer. Show me how I can change the world for Jesus. Amen.

JESUS GLOBE

God wants us to change our world for Jesus. Write three things you can start doing to change your world at home, school and in your neighborhood.

_____

_____

_____

GOTTA KNOW ABOUT ME

God has many plans for me.
But be glad and rejoice forever in what I will create.
Isaiah 65:18

God's Plans

"Look, Mom," called Randy as he waved an envelope in the air.

"What is it?" Mom asked.

"Ben's birthday party invitation! Every boy in our class is going," Randy shouted. "Ben is taking us to Skateland. Then, we'll go to the Pizza Palace for pizza and cake and ice cream."

"Ben's parents sure have made special plans for his birthday," said Mom.

"Can I go, Mom?" asked Randy.

"Sure," said Mom.

We plan special days to have fun with friends at parties. God made special plans to know you before you were born. He planned to make a place for you to live and grow. That is why God made the heavens and the earth. God loved you then, and He loves you now.

The Bible says we should be glad and rejoice in all God has created. Thank God that He planned to have a place for you and your family to live. Plan to know God as He has planned to know you.

Your Turn

1. How can you find out God's plans for you?
2. How can you help your friends find God's plan for them?

_____

_____

_____

_____

_____

_____

Prayer

Thank You, God, for the plans You have made for me. Thank You for Your plans to care for me. Help me follow Your plans for me. Amen.

PEEK AT MY WEEK

Draw a picture each day this week showing a friend you plan to invite over to play. Plan to tell your friend how God loves him or her and how He created the earth and everything on it. Plan to talk to God before bed each night.

GOTTA KNOW ABOUT ME

God knows all about me.
I am the good shepherd; I know my sheep and my sheep know me.
John 10:14-15

God and Me

Wil Bradford lives just down the street from me. His house is at the end of our block. His house isn't painted yet because it is brand new.

Wil is 8 years old — same as me. We are at the same school, Grover Elementary. He has a 15-year-old brother and a 2-year-old sister.

Wil's dad drives a new pick-up truck to work each day. His mother doesn't work and stays at home to watch Wil's little sister.

Wil has blond hair and blue eyes. Does it sound like I know Wil very well? I don't even know Wil Bradford! He doesn't know me. I see him playing in front of his house down the street. My friends tell me about his family. I know about him because I see him at school each day. I know facts about Wil Bradford, but I don't really know him.

Is there someone you only know about, but don't know well? What about God? God is like a shepherd who knows his sheep. You are like one of His sheep. Are you a sheep who knows your Shepherd?

Your Turn

1. What do you know about God?
2. How can you get to know God?
3. How do you act toward someone you know? How do you act toward God?

_____

_____

_____

_____

_____

_____

Prayer

I want to know You, God. If You are real, please show me. Amen.

KNOWING GOD'S HEART

Draw a picture of yourself inside the heart. At the bottom of the page, make a list of kids you know, but don't know well. Call someone from your list on the telephone. Invite them to your house after school or on the weekend.

_____

_____

_____

_____

GOTTA KNOW ABOUT GOD

God wants me to belong to Him.
Return to me for I have redeemed [to buy back] *you.*
Isaiah 44:22

I Belong to God

Cody left his bike out in the yard one night. When he woke up the next morning, the bike was gone. Someone had stolen it!

One day Cody was walking down the sidewalk. He passed a boy on a bike. As he passed the boy, he noticed the boy was riding Cody's bike. It was the bike that had been stolen!

Cody chased the boy hoping he could get his bike back. When he caught up with the boy, Cody asked him for his bike. The boy wouldn't return Cody's bike. So Cody said, "I'll give you ten dollars for that bike."

The boy said he would sell the bike back to Cody for ten dollars. The boy wanted the ten dollars more than he wanted the bike. Cody saved his bike and bought it back for himself.

Do you know that we were bought back by God? God made us and we belong to Him. But, we were taken away from God by not loving Him and making wrong choices. Doing things our way and not God's way is called sin. But, God bought us back from those things. He saved us! It is like the boy who bought his own bike back. Jesus died on the cross to buy us back for God. Jesus was the price God paid to get us back from sin. Anyone who wants to have Jesus as Lord and Savior can be bought back to be in God's big family.

Your Turn

1. To whom do we belong?
2. What did Jesus do to get us back to God?
3. Have you been bought back to be in God's big family?

_____

_____

_____

Prayer

Thank You, God, for wanting me even though I sometimes let the things of this world get in the way of loving You. Help me to remember how much You paid to have me as Your child. Amen.

THE SECRET BIKE CODE

Try to figure out the code in the bike spokes below. Put the words in the spokes under the right number to decode message. The answer is on page 231.

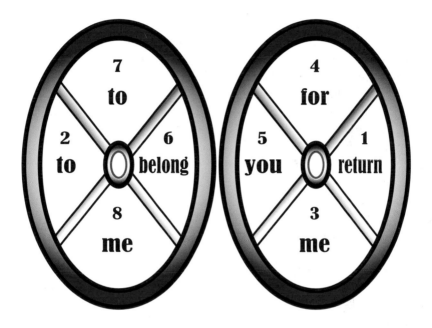

_____   _____   _____   _____
    1   **2**   **3**   **4**

_____   _____   _____   _____
  5   **6**   **7**   **8**

GOTTA KNOW
GOD'S MEN

ABRAHAM

It's good to follow God's ways.
He will teach us his ways.

Isaiah 2:3

Abraham Followed God

In Old Testament times, a special man named Abraham learned to follow God's ways. Abraham and his wife Sarah were happy living in a city called Ur. God had provided a nice home and everything they needed.

One day God suddenly surprised Abraham. God told him, "Leave Ur and move your home to a new country built by My hand."

Abraham listened as God gave him the message. He could have asked God many questions. "What place is this?" "How long will Sarah and I be there?" "What about leaving friends?" Abraham and Sarah had grown up in Ur. Ur was the only home they knew.

God told Abraham he wouldn't have a map to follow. "Just follow My voice," said the Lord. Abraham must have had many questions in his mind. But he knew how to follow God. Abraham had learned to follow and trust God without asking questions.

Could you learn to trust and follow God's way like Abraham? If God told your parents to move, would you be happy? Would you follow God?

Your Turn

1. How would you feel if your family had to move? Could you follow God even if you had to leave friends and family?
2. Do you think you love God enough to follow Him like Abraham did?

_____

_____

_____

_____

_____

Prayer

Dear God, I want to follow You like Abraham did. Teach me to trust You to lead me the right way. Amen.

ABRAHAM'S SUITCASE

Abraham had to move from his home to a strange place. What does following God mean to you? For example: reading your Bible, being kind to mean kids or being friends with people no one likes. Write your ideas on Abraham's suitcase.

ABRAHAM

God wants me to follow Him.
The ways of the Lord are right.

Hosea 14:9

I Follow God

Following the directions to a game makes the game fun and easy to play. Making paper airplanes instead of listening to your teacher will keep you from learning at school. Playing with your shoe strings instead of following the Bible class teacher will keep you from hearing God's Word. A football coach must be followed in order to play football the right way. Piano notes must be followed carefully to play a song right.

Following God's way is like playing the right notes to make a beautiful song. God wants you to follow Him so your life will come out right. When you forget to follow God's ways, things go wrong.

The Bible says, "The ways of the Lord are right." You can begin to follow God by reading the Bible and going to church.

You follow a map when you want to go down a road. The road signs on the map tell you where to go. As you get to know Him, He shows you the right way to go. Talking to God in prayer also helps you to know His ways. Joy and happiness always come when you follow God's ways.

Your Turn

1. Why should you follow your parents?
2. How does helping others show you are following God?
3. Think of a time when you didn't follow God at school, home or church. What can you do now to begin following God?

_____

_____

_____

_____

_____

Prayer

God, help me to learn to follow You at school, home and church. Show me how to follow You so I can live Your way. Amen.

GOD'S MAP

Following God's way is like following a good map — taking the right roads to get you to the right place. Write on the street signs below ways to follow God at school and home. Examples: Bible Reading, God's Ten Rules.

NOAH

God likes for me to give Him thanks.
Praise the Lord, for the Lord is good.

Psalm 135:3

Noah Thanked God

Todd couldn't wait to get out of the family van. Riding in the car for three hours with a crying baby sister hadn't been much fun.

"What's the first thing you will do when we get home?" Dad asked Todd. "I'm going to see if one of the kids can play basketball," Todd said.

"That reminds me of Noah in the Bible," said Mom. "I'll bet Noah's family couldn't wait to get home from their trip. Can you imagine riding for 150 days with monkeys, giraffes and bears?"

"Tell me more about Noah," said Todd.

Mom turned her head and spoke softly. "Noah and his family were glad they were safe inside the ark when it started to rain. It rained and rained! The water went higher and higher. Soon everything on earth was covered with water. After a long time, the water went down again. Finally it was time when everyone could leave the ark. Noah's family and the animals came off the ark. Right away the animals ran and jumped around. But Noah and his family didn't run and jump. Noah had something special to do first. Noah picked up some big stones. He built a place to worship God right next to the ark. Noah praised God and thanked Him for keeping his family safe. What do you think of Noah and his thankfulness?"

"Maybe we should thank God for getting us home safely," said Todd.

"I thought you wanted to play basketball," said Dad.

"I think it would make God happier if we stopped to thank Him for getting us home safely first," said Todd.

Your Turn

1. What important thing did Noah do on land?
2. Where can you give thanks to God?

Prayer

Dear God, thank You for taking good care of me. You keep me safe at home and church. You're even with me on the playground when I climb with my friends. Thank You, God. Amen.

ARK OF THANKFULNESS

In the ark below draw a picture of something for which you are thankful. Look up the word "altar" in the dictionary. Build (draw) your own rock altar for worship below the ark.

NOAH

I love to thank God.
Praise the Lord. O my soul, and forget not all his benefits.
Isaiah 48:17

I'll Thank God

"What happened?" Ben asked as Mom hung up the phone.

"Mr. Rider said Bryan ran his bike into the fence over at Dinosaur Hill," answered Mom. "He got going too fast and couldn't stop. But he wasn't hurt badly."

"I wonder if he was wearing his helmet?" asked Ben.

"He was!" said Mom. "The doctor told Mr. Rider that the helmet is what saved him. He only had to have three stitches above his left eye. It could have been a lot worse."

Mom smiled. "God is so great to have kept him from harm."

"I ride my bike over that hill almost every day. I've never run into that fence," said Ben. "I don't think it was the helmet that saved Bryan."

Ben pointed upward. "I think God protected Bryan."

Mom shook her head in agreement. "I guess we forget to thank God for His protection. We only want to give thanks when something bad almost happens."

"Maybe we should thank God more for keeping us safe," said Ben.

The Bible says to give thanks in all things (see 1 Thessalonians 5:16). So even bad things can be a blessing to God's people. But we should never forget all His goodness to us. What a great God we have!

Your Turn

1. What can you do to thank God more often?
2. What are some things that have happened to you for which can give thanks to God?

_____

_____

_____

Prayer

Thank You, God, for all the love and care You give us each day. Thank You for being good to us even when we forget to give thanks for the good things that happen. Help me not to forget You, God. Amen.

DINOSAUR HILL

Write a note to God on the dinosaur's back. Thank Him for something new He has done for you.

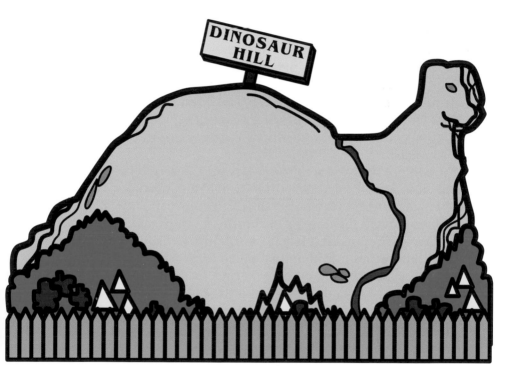

REUBEN

Showing goodness is helpful.
Trust in the Lord and do good.
Psalm 37:3

Reuben's Goodness

Jason showed goodness to his baby sister by helping Mom rock her to sleep.

Cory showed goodness to his brother after the boy fell off his bike. Cory helped him stand up and gave him a hug.

Reuben, a boy in Bible times, showed kindness to his younger brother Joseph. Joseph's 11 brothers hated him. The brothers thought their father loved Joseph more than them.

To make matters worse, Joseph had a dream. He told his brothers about it. "We were making piles of wheat in the field," he said. "My pile of wheat stood up. Your piles of wheat came all around mine. They bowed down to mine."

"We will not bow down to you," they said. Joseph's brothers hated him.

One day Joseph's dad called for him. "Your brothers are in the fields caring for the sheep. See if everything is going well with them."

So Joseph went looking for his brothers. They saw him coming before he got there. They made plans to kill him by throwing him into a well. "We'll tell our father a wild animal killed him," they said.

Joseph's oldest brother Reuben tried to save Joseph. "Let's not kill him. Throw him into a dry well," said Reuben. "But don't kill him."

Reuben planned to come back later and take Joseph home. Reuben had shown goodness to his brother Joseph. God loves to see goodness in you. God notices when you show your goodness to others.

Your Turn

1. Would you show goodness to someone even if your friends didn't want to?
2. What does it mean to do good to others?
3. How can you help others to do good?

Prayer

Dear God, show me how to do good like Reuben. Help me to do good so others will want to do good. Amen.

GOODNESS WELL

The Bible says, "Trust in the Lord and do good." Think of people you know to whom you can show goodness. Write their names on the lines next to the well below.

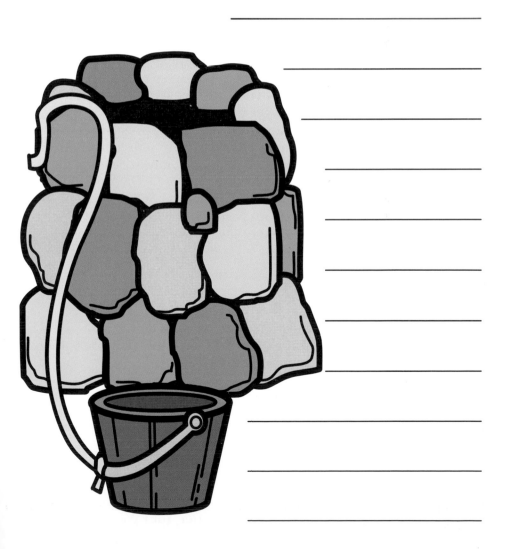

REUBEN

God wants me to show goodness.
Let us not become weary in doing good.

Galatians 6:9

A Good Job!

Jerry was responsible for taking the evening newspaper to 30 of his neighbors each day. He was careful not to throw the papers into the bushes or anywhere else. Most of the other paper boys and girls threw their papers from a moving car. Their papers landed on the driveways or in people's yards.

Jerry wanted to do a good job. His parents always told him to do his work as if he were doing it for Jesus. Folding 30 papers after school each day was hard. He even had to put a rubber band around each one. When it rained he had to also place them into a bag.

Jerry was tired some days. On cold, snowy days he put on his boots. He would march in deep snow to get papers to his neighbors.

The neighbors didn't thank Jerry for doing such a good job for them. He never got many tips. At Christmas time only four neighbors tipped him! They didn't notice his goodness. But Jerry never gave up! He never got tired of doing good for others and God.

Would Jesus ever get tired of doing good for us? When we disobey Him He keeps forgiving us and helping us. Jesus doesn't get tired of doing good things for us. Jesus never gets tired of loving us. We shouldn't get tired of doing good things for others either.

Your Turn

1. What good things make you tired?
2. What should you do when you become tired of doing good?
3. How do you think Jesus felt about what Jerry was doing for others?
4. Can you think of ways Jesus is good to you?

_____

_____

_____

Prayer

Dear Jesus, thank You for not getting tired of loving me. Help me to do good to others and obey You. Help me to notice Your goodness. Amen.

THE GOODNESS HEADLINES

Make up your own newspaper goodness headline below. Think of ways you can show the goodness of God to others. Write your name in the first space. Write what you are doing or plan to do in the next spaces.

Daily Herald

_____
(your name)

DID NOT GROW WEARY OF DOING GOOD. HE _____ AND _____.

MOSES

God loves faithfulness.
*Well done, good and faithful servant! You have been
faithful with a few things.*

Matthew 25:21

Moses, A Faithful Hero

Moses was a faithful hero. God gave him big, important jobs! He knew Moses would be faithful with the jobs He gave him.

Moses could be faithful to God because he knew God would always help him. God told Moses to tell the king of Egypt to let His people go free. The people were being used as slaves to do the king's work.

God said to Moses. "I'm sending you to the king of Egypt. Tell him to let My people go!"

At first, Moses didn't want to do it! "Send someone else," said Moses. "I'm not the man for this important job." Moses was afraid to speak to the king. He had a stuttering problem and didn't think he could speak well enough to make the king let God's people go.

God knew He could help Moses be faithful to sway the king. He told Moses what to say to the king. "Here, take this walking stick," said God. Moses used the stick to show the king what God can do. God had given Moses this tool to help him be faithful to do the job.

Moses was faithful to use the stick each time God told him to. Once he threw the stick on the ground and it turned into a snake. Another time Moses stretched out his arm with the stick. He placed the tip of it in the river and the water turned to blood. After Moses did everything God said to do with the stick, God's people were free.

Moses was one of God's heroes because he was faithful to God. God loved Moses and was proud of him for being faithful.

Your Turn

1. Why was Moses a faithful hero in God's eyes?
2. How can you be a faithful hero for God?

_____

_____

Prayer

Lord help me to be faithful like Moses. Help me to be faithful in doing what You and my parents ask me to do. Amen.

MY FAITHFUL STAFF

Draw a staff in the boy's hand below to remind you to always be faithful to God. At the bottom of page write something you can be faithful to do for God.

_____

_____

_____

MOSES

God helps me to be a leader for Him.
Teach me your ways, O Lord; lead me in a straight path.

Psalm 27:11

I'm God's Leader

Three boys ran down a winding dirt path. They came to a fork in the path. (A fork is a place where another path appears.) A dark forest with many trees could be seen down the new path.

Where does this path lead? the boys wondered. Having never been down that path before they weren't sure if it was safe.

Maybe it's a short cut back to our houses, they thought.

Two of the boys said they were sure the new path went by the lake. They knew the main path ended up in their neighborhood.

"Which path should we take?" the boys asked each other. "Someone has to be the leader."

"I'll lead," said a boy named Todd. "But I think something is strange about that path at the fork. Let's stay on the main path."

"But we like adventure," said the other two boys. "Let's take the fork to the dark forest."

"Let's go," said the two boys. Todd shook his head. He wasn't so sure! "No!" he said. "Follow me and I will lead you home by the main path." The two boys looked at Todd and then each other. "Well, maybe we should go back by the main path after all," they said. The boys turned around and Todd led them safely home.

Sometimes others want to lead you the wrong way. You can always say no and do what is safe and right. That is what Todd did and the others followed him.

Your Turn

1. Have you ever been led to do the wrong thing? What happened?
2. How can God help you to lead others the right way?

Prayer

Dear God teach me to lead the right way. Help me to be a good leader for You. Amen.

THE LEADING FEET

Write your name on each of the feet below that leads to good behavior.
"Jump over" feet that do not lead to good behavior.

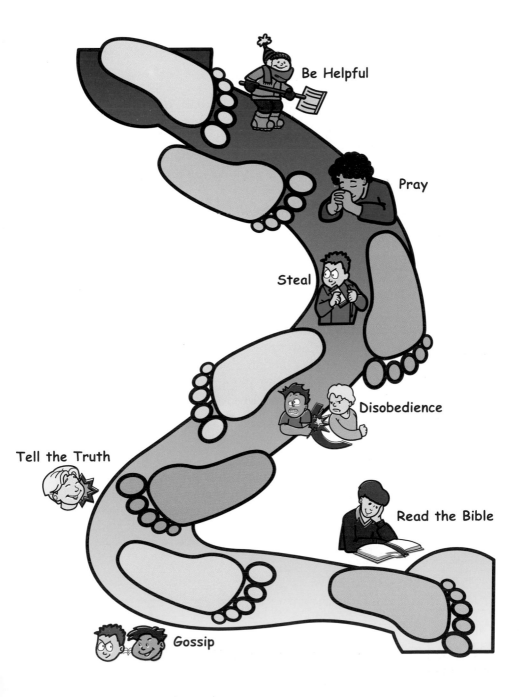

Be Helpful

Pray

Steal

Disobedience

Tell the Truth

Read the Bible

Gossip

MOSES

God is looking for faithful kids.
*Many a man claims to have unfailing love,
but a faithful man who can find?*

Proverbs 20:6

A Faithful Player

"It's too bad Nick Justin is leaving basketball. He is the greatest player that ever lived," Mitch told his dad and brother Alec.

Mitch held the magazine story about Nick Justin in his hands. "It says right here that Nick never missed a game. 'Players and coaches describe him as being a very hard worker' it says. 'He is known for doing what his coaches asked of him.' "

"God honors a faithful man," said Dad. "You guys know that Nick Justin is a believer in Christ, don't you? Many times he has spoken out about it on the Sports Channel."

"Wow! I forgot about that," said Mitch. "That explains why I have never seen him arguing with the ref."

"God has blessed Justin's talent because he is faithful to Him," said Dad.

You don't have to be a famous basketball player to be faithful to God. You can be a faithful player anytime or anywhere. Being faithful to God means obeying your parents or keeping your room neat. Being a faithful player means playing fairly on the playground at school. Sharing and being kind is being a faithful player for God. Are you a faithful player for God?

Your Turn

1. Can you think of ways to be a faithful player for God?
2. Look up the word "faithful" in the dictionary. What does it mean?
3. Why is God looking for faithful kids? Are you one?

_____

_____

_____

Prayer

God, make me a faithful kid. Help me to do my best at all I do. Keep me faithful to You as I clean my room and love my family. Amen.

THE SPORTS SHIRT

Draw how you can be faithful to God on the sports shirt below.

JOSHUA

Knowing God makes me brave.
Be strong and courageous [brave].

Deuteronomy 31:7

Joshua's Brave Heart

"I can't be your leader anymore. I am too old," said Moses. "Joshua will lead you now. God will go in front of you to protect you."

God began to speak to Joshua, "Be strong! Be brave! I will help you to lead My people to the Promised Land [their special place]."

When Moses died, Joshua became one of God's heroes. God's people were worried about going into the new land. No one knew what might be waiting for them there. Mean kings might be in the new land. What if there was no food or water in the new land?

Joshua's heart was brave in going to the new land. He knew God would help His people fight any enemy. Joshua trusted God to give the people food and water.

Just to be safe, Joshua sent spies out to see who was in the new land. The spies returned to Joshua and reported that the people in the new land were afraid of God's people. Joshua knew the land would belong to God's people, just as God said.

Joshua was never afraid of what might happen. Joshua knew God. Knowing God can help you to have a brave heart. A brave heart will help you do the things God wants you to do.

Your Turn

1. What made Joshua so brave?
2. Do you think Joshua was ever afraid? Why or why not?

_____

_____

_____

_____

_____

Prayer

Dear Lord, help me to have a brave heart like Joshua. Let others know I am brave because I know You, God. Amen.

A BRAVE HEART

Color a picture or write inside the heart an act you wish to be more brave in doing. Ask God to give you a brave heart.

JOSHUA

God helps me to be brave.
Stand firm in the faith; be men of courage; be strong.
1 Corinthians 16:13

My Brave Heart

Mrs. Hansen's second grade had been planning their class picnic for weeks. They had decided to make peanut butter and honey sandwiches in class the morning of the picnic. Each child would bring their own drink. Parents were making the sugar cookies for desert.

The class would follow the new bike path behind the school to the new Adventure Park and playground. The park was one mile up the hill, around the corner and over a foot bridge. Mrs. Hansen's class had not been to Adventure Park because it had just opened.

Cory Bryan was chosen to lead his class to the picnic area. He was very scared thinking about leading the whole class down the path to the new playground. He knew it was a great honor to be chosen to lead the class.

What would they see along the way? What if something bad happened? he thought. He wanted to have a brave heart and be sure about it, but Cory wasn't feeling brave.

Mrs. Hansen could see that Cory was worried. She put her arm around him. "Did you know God wants to help you to be brave? His Word tells us to be people of courage and be strong," she said. "Let's pray and ask God to help us as we go to the new playground."

Cory sighed. "My heart is feeling brave already. With God helping me I know I can be brave in leading the class."

"I will also be there to help," said Mrs. Hansen.

Your Turn

1. What does it mean to be brave?
2. How can God help you to be brave for Him?

_____

_____

_____

Prayer

Dear God, teach me to be brave for You. Show me how to trust You to take care of me. Amen.

ADVENTURE PARK SLIDE MAZE

Start at the top of the slide with a crayon and follow Cory down the slide. (Cory is brave because he now knows that God will help him to be brave.)

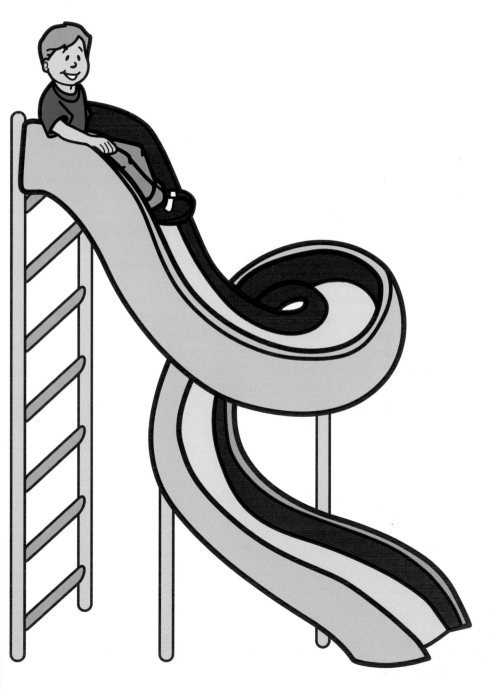

SAMUEL

Samuel heard God's voice at night.
To obey the Lord is better than an offering.

1 Samuel 15:22

A Night Call

"Samuel! Samuel!" The sound rang in Samuel's ears when he slept. Samuel was used to hearing Eli, the priest who was in charge of Samuel's training about God. Samuel had lived with Eli since he was 3. When Samuel heard God's voice, he thought it was Eli. "I'm right here," said Samuel. He ran to where Eli was sleeping and asked, "You called me?"

"I didn't call to you," said Eli. "Go back to bed."

Samuel went back to bed. But soon he heard "Samuel!" God had never talked to Samuel. Samuel got up again and went to Eli. "You called for me?" he asked. "Go back to bed," said Eli.

Then suddenly Eli realized that God was calling Samuel. He told Samuel that if he heard God again to say to Him, "I am listening." So Samuel went back to bed. He wasn't sleeping long when God said, "Samuel!"

"I am listening," he repeated.

"I am going to surprise many people," said God. "I am going to judge Eli's family. Eli knew his boys were doing wrong and he didn't stop them."

The next morning, Samuel heard Eli call his name.

"What did God tell you, Samuel?" he asked. Samuel was afraid to tell Eli. "Don't hide God's words from me," said Eli. Samuel told Eli what God said.

Eli said, "Let God do what He thinks is best."

Samuel was glad he heard God's voice. He couldn't wait to hear God's voice again. He became a great man for God. God continued to tell Samuel many things to pass on to the people.

Your Turn

1. Would you have been scared if you had heard God's voice?
2. Do you think we can hear God's voice in the same way Samuel did?
3. After you hear God's voice, what should you do next?

_____

_____

Prayer

God, help me to hear Your voice and obey You. Amen.

MY ANSWERS TO GOD

Eli told Samuel that God was calling him. Samuel answered God's voice and God made him a special man before the people. Pretend like you are hearing God's voice. Write your name in the voice box from God. Write in the box what your answer to God should be.

(your name)_____

My answer to God: _____
_____
_____
_____
_____

SAMUEL

God wants us to hear from Him.
Listen to his voice and hold fast to him, for the Lord is your life.
Deuteronomy 30:20

Hearing from God

"Bradley!" called Mom. Bradley sat staring straight ahead as he watched "The Rocket Man Adventure" on TV.

"Bradley! Bradley!" called Mom for a second time. Bradley still didn't hear Mom over the sound of the TV. Mom walked over and turned off the TV. Bradley jumped from the bean bag chair.

"Did you call me, Mom?" asked Bradley.

"Yes!" said Mom. "I called you many times. You weren't able to hear me because of the TV."

"What do you want me to do?" he asked.

"It is almost time for your baseball practice," she said. "You'd better get changed and grab your ball and glove."

"Oh! I didn't know it was so late," said Bradley. "Thanks for calling me." "You know, Brad," said Mom, "TV may keep you from hearing something really important next time."

"You mean I shouldn't ever watch TV?" asked Brad.

"No, that's not what I mean," said Mom. "I just think you need to learn how to be still and listen. Don't let TV be so important to you."

It is a good thing Samuel wasn't watching TV when God called to him. God wants us to be able to hear His voice. Find time to sit and listen for God.

Your Turn

1. What can you do to be sure you hear God's voice?
2. Have you heard from God?

_____

_____

_____

_____

Prayer

God, help me to turn off the TV and video games to hear from You. Let me learn to hear Your voice and obey You. Amen.

BASEBALL TRAVEL

What keeps you from hearing God's voice? Write down those things as you travel around the bases below. Write your name on home base, where God will call to you.

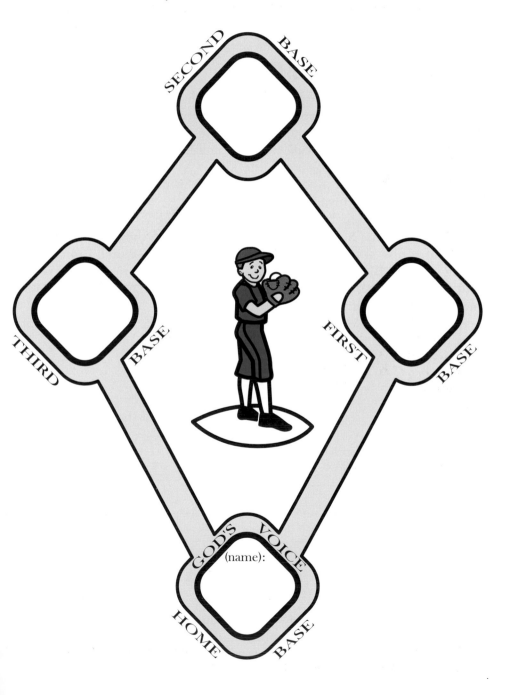

DAVID

I worship God because He is so great.
Worship the Lord with gladness; come before
Him with joyful songs.

Psalm 100:2

David Worshipped God

David was one of the greatest kings to rule over God's people. David's music made him great in God's eyes. As a shepherd boy, David would sing to his sheep when he watched over them.

David played the harp well. So King Saul invited him into his court to play for him. He played to soothe the king.

David loved God so much that it made him want to sing. The joy he felt for God made him want to dance.

Years later when he became a man, David wrote 73 songs to God. They were called psalms. Now the psalms of David are in the Bible.

David's trust in God made him want to worship. Worshipping God is saying you love Him. When David worshipped God, he told Him, "You are kind, loving, forgiving and caring." David lifted his hands to the sky and told God he loved Him.

Worshipping God is thanking Him and loving Him. Some people worship God as they listen to God's music. You can worship God anywhere and anytime.

Your Turn

1. Read Psalm 23 in the Bible. What does David call the Lord in that passage?
2. Why did David want to worship God?

_____

_____

_____

_____

Prayer

Dear Lord, You are my God. I worship You and thank You for caring for me. Thank You for being my Shepherd. I don't need anything if I have You. Amen.

MY PSALM

On the music lines below, write your own psalm to God. When you worship Him, sing your psalm to Him.

DAVID

I love worshipping God.
Come let us bow down in worship, let us kneel
before the Lord our Maker.

Psalm 95:6

Worship Is Fun

Eating ice cream is fun! Riding a roller coaster is fun! Spending the day at Grandma's is fun. A holiday party is fun.

Birthday parties are fun because you play games and sing songs. Birthdays honor people on the special day of their birth. We honor people on their birthdays because we love them.

Christmas parties honor Jesus on His birthday because we love Him. Fourth of July parties honor our country because we love our country. Worshipping God is like a party. It is a time when we honor God and Jesus. We honor them because they love us and we love them. Worshipping is like having a special party to thank God and Jesus. We thank them for the many things they have done. They watch over us, forgive us and help us.

Worshipping God and Jesus is like having a party to say, "I love you!" That is why we worship! There are many kinds of birthday parties. Some birthday parties are with just family members. Other parties are with many friends and lots of games.

Worship is like that. You can worship in a quiet place just to think about God. You can worship listening to music. The music can be fast or slow. You can lift your hands toward heaven. You can carry banners or instruments. Waving the banners is like waving flags for Jesus. Worshipping God is fun!

Your Turn

1. Why do you worship God and Jesus?
2. How is worship fun?
3. What are some ways to worship?

Prayer

Dear God, I want to worship You. I am glad I can worship You. I am glad I can worship Jesus. Amen.

BANNER OF FUN

Color your worship banner below. Draw something on the banner that reminds you of God.

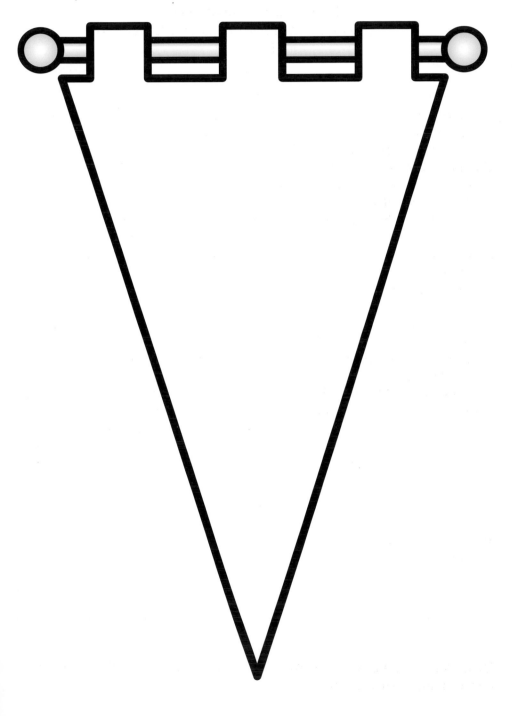

SOLOMON

It is good to be in God's house.
I rejoiced with those who said to me,
"Let us go to the house of the Lord."

Psalm 122:1

Solomon and God's House

Solomon was King David's son. When David got old, he made his son king.

David had taught Solomon to love God's house. Solomon wanted to build a beautiful temple for God. He wanted the temple to be a special place where people could come to worship God. Solomon made great plans to build God's house.

A nearby king sent men to help his friend Solomon build the temple. When the great house of God was built, Solomon called all of the people to come to the temple. He wanted them to worship God by singing, dancing and praying.

The people needed a place to go where they could tell God how they felt. People came to the temple to worship God from near and far. Fathers, mothers, boys and girls all came to the temple.

Solomon was happy when he saw all the people coming to worship God. He lifted his hands to the sky and said, "There is no God like you. God, You are so great! God, hear the prayers of Your people from this place of worship."

Your Turn

1. Why did Solomon want to build a temple?
2. Who listened to Solomon when he prayed?
3. Why did so many people go to Solomon's temple?

_____

_____

_____

_____

Prayer

Dear God, there is no God like You. You are so great! Hear my prayers each day. Amen.

MY TEMPLE

Build your own temple around the boy praying below.

SOLOMON

God wants me to enjoy His house.
Blessed are those who dwell in your house.

Psalm 84:4

The Tree House

A.J. helped his dad build a tree house behind their house. He spent every afternoon playing in the tree house. The neighbor kids also loved to play in the tree house. A.J. liked sharing the tree house.

But the quiet times in the tree house were the best. He loved being alone, too. Just sitting and thinking was fun to him.

One Sunday morning A.J. awoke early. He climbed the tree house to play. He was placing the army men in a line when a voice rang out.

"A.J.! it's time to get dressed for church," called Mom.

"I want to stay and play in my tree house today," he yelled back.

Mom walked over to the tree house. She stood at the base and looked upward. "You love your tree house, don't you?" she asked A.J.

"Yes!" said A.J. Mom climbed a few steps up the tree house ladder. She stuck her head in a tree house window.

"God wants us to love His house, too," she said. "Sunday is called the Lord's day! We set aside Sunday as a special day to honor Him in His house, the church."

"Isn't every day God's special day?" asked A.J.

"Well, it is," said Mom. "But part of loving God is going to His house on Sundays. Getting together with God's people pleases Him. Your tree house is nice, but God's house is best. Now, will you come down and get changed for church? We'll be late if we don't hurry."

"I guess God's house is where I should be on Sundays," said A.J. "Look out! Here I come," he said.

Your Turn

1. Why does God want you to go to His house on Sunday?

2. Why is God's house special to you?

Prayer

Dear God, thank You for Your house. Teach me to love Your house more than playing with toys. Teach me to love Your house more than those things. Amen.

MY TREE HOUSE

What would you rather do than go to church? Write those things on the tree house below. Tell God you're sorry for putting your house ahead of His house. Color the picture.

GIDEON

God wants soldiers for His army.
You did not choose Me, but I chose you.

John 15:16

Gideon's Win

"God, are you really choosing me?" asked Gideon.

Gideon told people what God said. Gideon trusted God.

God knew Gideon believed Him, so God let Gideon lead an army against the Midianites. The Midianites were bothering the people of God. They kept taking land away from God's people, the Israelites. Gideon planned to fight Midian with a big, big army.

God said to Gideon, "You have too many men in your army. When your army wins they will say that they won because they are strong."

God wanted Gideon's army to know that He alone would help them win. God told Gideon to tell any who were afraid to go home. Many men left and went home.

"There are still too many men," said God. "Take your men to the stream and let them drink. Some men will scoop water with their hands and lap it like dogs. Other men will get on their knees and drink from the stream. Take the men who lap the water like a dog. These 300 men will be your army. The other men may go home."

Gideon and his small army went to fight Midian at night. The men marched, blew trumpets and carried torches. God made the Midianites get mixed up. They killed each other! Gideon listened to God and believed God would help the army win. That is why God chose Gideon.

Your Turn

1. Would God choose you to lead an army for Him? Why or why not?
2. What could you do in God's army?
3. How has God helped you do something for Him?

_____

_____

_____

Prayer

Thank You, God, for letting me be a soldier in Your army. I am glad You chose me. Give me Your directions and teach me to follow You. Amen.

THE SOLDIERS

God chooses you to be a leader for Him. Draw yourself at the start of the army line (under the L for "leader") to remind you that God wants to chose you to be a leader.

GIDEON

God wants Jesus to be your captain.
A soldier wants to please his captain.

2 Timothy 3:4

My Captain

"Look at these soldier guys, Mom," said Alex. "I think I'll make this one a captain of all the guys and these guys will be at the front of the army. I'm going to put these soldiers in the middle of the army."

"Oh, that sounds like quite a big army," said Mom. "Here, you can use this box as a fort for your guys."

"Thanks, Mom," said Alex. "My soldiers are going to do everything their captain tells them to do."

Alex made his captain give directions: "You guys hide in the trees over there." He placed them behind the curtain hanging from the window. "You go behind the rocks."

Alex placed more soldiers next to the pillow on the bed. "When I say go, everyone attack the enemy," called Alex. "One, two, three, go," he yelled. Alex made the men behind the curtain run to the middle of the room. Next he pulled the men from behind the pillow into the center of the room. Alex made his men win the battle because they listened to the voice of their captain. The men hid and waited until the right time to surprise the enemy.

When you obey God's Words in the Bible, you are obeying your captain. When you obey your parents, you obey your captain. You always win in God's eyes when you follow Him. You win every time you make God your captain.

Your Turn

1. Who is captain at your house?
2. How is God your captain?

_____

_____

_____

Prayer

Dear God, help me to hear my captain's voice and obey Him. Teach me to obey my parents so my captain will be pleased. Amen.

CAPTAIN'S HAT

Draw a picture below the helmet of something your captain God has told you to do. It may be something your parents told you to do, too. Did you obey and do it?

JESUS

Jesus is my favorite hero.
*There is but one Lord, Jesus Christ, through whom
all things came and through whom we live.*

1 Corinthians 8:6

My Favorite Hero!

"Who is your favorite superhero?" asked Kevin's Sunday school teacher. "Superman!" called Kevin.

"Jesus is mine," said Brittany.

"Is He sort of like a Superman with long hair and a hairy chin?" asked Kevin.

"No! He's nothing like that," replied Brittany. "Superman is fun to watch on TV, but he's a cartoon hero. He isn't real. Jesus is real."

"Superman fights crime and gets the bad guys," said Kevin. "What does Jesus do?"

"He is real and lives in heaven with God, His father," she said. "Jesus is kind and loving to all people. It doesn't matter how they look or where they live, He loves them. Jesus doesn't get angry easily. He fights with words from the Bible, not His feet or fists."

"What else do you know about this hero, Jesus?" asked Kevin.

"He is sad when we do wrong, but ready to forgive when we are sorry," Brittany replied. The teacher then told Kevin how Jesus wants to be his number one hero.

"How can Jesus be my hero?" asked Kevin.

The teacher put her arm around Kevin. "Jesus came to earth and died to pay for the wrong things we do. He paid for our selfishness. But God brought Jesus back to life. He lives forever and wants to be a hero for you too. You can start letting Him be your hero by loving and obeying Him."

"I guess Superman isn't my favorite hero after all," said Kevin.

Your Turn

1. What makes Jesus the best hero ever?
2. Do you want Jesus as your hero? Pray and ask Him to be your hero.

Prayer

Dear God, thank You for Jesus. I pray You will help me to look to Him to be my hero and not Superman. Amen.

SUPER HEROES

On the back of Jesus' cape below, write your favorite heroes. Are they as wonderful as Jesus?

JESUS

I can put others first, like Jesus.
Honor one another above yourselves.

Romans 12:10

What Would Jesus Do?

There were two boys who waited the same length of time for the Zinger roller coaster ride. When time came to get onto the ride, there was room for only one of the boys. How should they decide who rides first?

Two boys arrive at the hot dog stand at the same time. Who should order first?

Your dad and mom ask you to help clean up the dinner dishes while your favorite TV show is about to begin. What should you do?

Choosing to put others first isn't always easy. If you aren't sure what to do, ask yourself a question: "What would Jesus do?" The answer will usually be that Jesus would put others first. Jesus wouldn't go ahead of the boy on the Zinger. Letting others be first in line and putting others ahead of yourself pleases God. Thinking of other people's needs before your own is one way to be happy.

When you don't put others first, you're being selfish. Jesus would never hurt someone's feelings in order to be first. If you don't know if you should go first, then ask yourself, "What would Jesus do?" Then putting others first will be easier for you.

Your Turn

1. Why should you put others first?
2. What do you call someone who only thinks of himself?
3. What should you do when someone doesn't put you first?

Prayer

Dear God, help me to remember to put other people first. I want to do what Jesus would do and put others first. Thank You, God, for putting me first in Your life. Teach me to put You first, God. Amen.

THE ROLLER COASTER PUZZLE

Let your friend go first on the roller coaster below. Find and circle the words, "What Would Jesus Do?" They are hidden in the letters on the roller coaster ride below. The answer is on page 231.

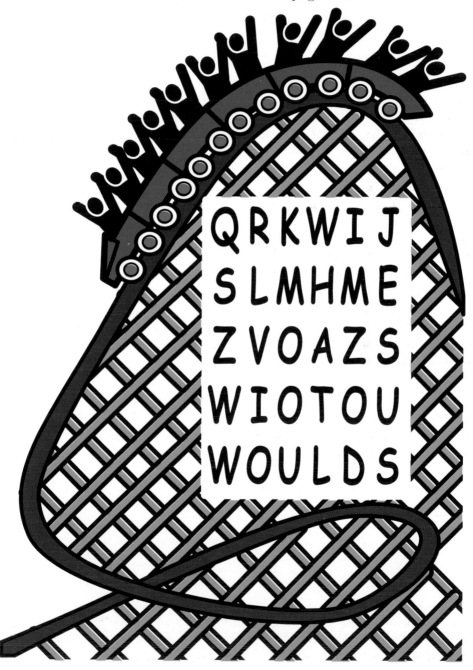

QRKWIJ
SLMHME
ZVOAZS
WIOTOU
WOULDS

JESUS

I can follow in the steps of Jesus.
Christ suffered for you, leaving you an example,
that you should follow in His steps.

1 Peter 2:21

Steps in the Sand

Chris and his dad walked up and down the beach gathering sand dollars.

"Dad, I'm stepping in your sand prints!" said Chris. He had been following his dad along the beach. Chris was trying to place his feet where his dad's feet had been.

Chris liked to follow the things his dad did. His dad liked to fish, so Chris liked to fish. His dad liked to build bird houses with a hammer and saw. Chris liked to build with a hammer and saw too.

Chris found he could follow his dad's steps in many things. When you do the things Jesus did, you are following in His steps. Obeying your parents is following in Jesus' steps. Showing kindness and being truthful is following in Jesus' steps. Helping and caring is following in Jesus' steps too. Whenever you do what Jesus would do, you are following in His steps.

Jesus gave you His footprints for you to walk in. Look inside the Bible! The steps of Jesus are there. You can follow His steps.

Your Turn

1. What are some of the things Jesus did on the earth?
2. Who can help you follow Jesus?
3. How does the Bible help you follow Jesus's steps?

_____

_____

_____

_____

_____

Prayer

Dear Jesus, thank You for Your good examples. Help me to follow You. Show me how to follow Your steps, Jesus. Amen.

SAND PRINTS

Follow Jesus' steps. Color each of Jesus' footprints in the sand to the end. Skip the footprints that aren't those of Jesus. The answer is on page 231.

JESUS

God wants me to copy Jesus.
*Be imitators of God, therefore, as dearly loved children,
and live a life of love, just as Christ loved us.*
Ephesians 5:1

Copying Jesus

Have you ever been called a copycat? A copycat is someone who does something just like someone else.

Your voice can be copied on a tape player. In "Follow the Leader," one person acts something out and another person copies him or her.

The Bible says Jesus did good things. Wherever Jesus went, He did good. Wherever you go you can do good, too. You can copy Jesus! Jesus healed the sick. You can put your arm around a sick person for God to heal him or her. You can cheer up someone who is sick. Jesus gave hungry people something to eat. You can help feed people who are hungry. Jesus helped people learn about God. You can copy Jesus and talk to children and grown-ups about God and Jesus.

Is there someone you can invite to church today? Jesus did many good things. You can copy Jesus and do many good things too. You can be a copycat for Jesus!

Your Turn

1. What can you do to copy Jesus?
2. What does the Scripture above say about Jesus?
3. What are some good things Jesus did?

_____

_____

_____

_____

_____

_____

Prayer

Dear Jesus, I want to be like You. Help me to do good like Jesus did. Amen.

JESUS SAYS GAME

Instead of playing "Simon Says" play "Jesus Says." Draw a line from the boy to the pictures that show how to copy Jesus. Put an x over the pictures that don't copy Jesus. The answer is on page 231.

PETER

Jesus is looking for willing workers.
Jesus said, "I will make you fishers of men."

Mark 1:17

Fishing

Jesus wanted to find 12 good men to help Him with His work on earth. One day, Jesus walked beside the lake. He looked and saw two fishermen, Peter and Andrew. They were throwing their fishing nets into the water to catch fish. Jesus called to them, "Come follow Me. I want to make you fishers of men." Right then they stopped fishing and followed Jesus.

That day, Peter became a special friend to Jesus. Peter learned to trust Jesus. Much later, after Jesus' resurrection, Peter was fishing, but he wasn't catching any fish. Jesus, who had returned to earth, called to him from the shore: "Throw your net on the other side of the boat."

When Peter obeyed, he caught more fish than he could haul in! Jesus cooked fish on the shore while Peter hauled in his fish. After they ate breakfast together, Jesus asked, "Peter, do you love Me?"

Peter said, "Yes."

"Then follow Me and care for My people," said Jesus.

Jesus returned to be with God in heaven. Peter missed Jesus, but he knew Jesus wanted him to be strong and tell others about Him. That is why Jesus surprised Peter with His visit. Peter did tell others about Him and he healed the sick in His name. Peter was a worker for Jesus.

Your Turn

1. What did Peter do when Jesus first called to him?
2. What should you do when Jesus wants you to do something for Him?
3. Peter was willing to tell others about Jesus. Are you willing to tell others about Jesus?

_____

_____

_____

Prayer

Dear Jesus, I pray You will help me to obey and follow You. Help me to tell others about You. Amen.

THE FISHING NET

Draw yourself inside the boat below. Fill the net next to the boat by coloring the fish to remind you to obey Jesus.

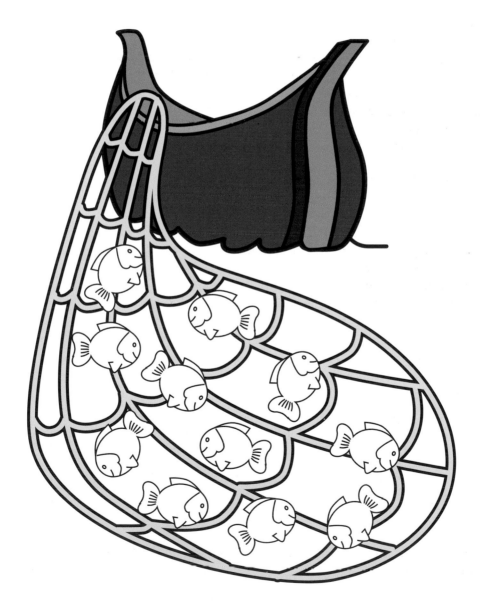

PETER

I am a willing worker.
Serve the Lord with gladness.

Psalm 100:2

Hard Work

"What's Brandon doing?" asked Brandon's little sister Ally.

"He's helping Mother," said Dad. Dad went into the kitchen to ask Mother a question. He noticed Brandon wasn't really helping. Brandon's head hung down and he was whispering to himself.

"Well, well," said Dad, "something must be wrong, Brandon. You don't seem happy helping Mom."

"No," said Brandon. "I'm not happy helping Mom."

"O.K.," said Dad, "I'll finish drying the dishes for you if you'll listen to a Bible verse."

Brandon thought that was fine. "What's the verse?" asked Brandon when Dad was done drying the dishes.

"It's Psalm 100, verse 2," replied Dad.

"I'll read it," said Brandon as he opened a Bible. " 'Serve the Lord with gladness.' "

"How do you serve the Lord?" asked Dad.

"With gladness," said Brandon. "I guess I wasn't very glad when I helped Mom with the dishes, was I?"

"I guess you didn't do it this time, Brandon. But I know you can serve the Lord with gladness next time."

"I'm sorry," said Brandon. "Next time I'll try to be happy about it. I do want to be a willing worker for Jesus."

Dad put his arm around Brandon. "Working hard for Jesus is good. Helping your mom with the dishes is being a willing worker for Jesus."

Your Turn

1. How did Brandon show he wasn't a willing worker?
2. Why did Brandon want to be a willing worker the next time?

_____

_____

Prayer

Dear Jesus, I am glad You are my God and Savior. Help me remember that I can serve You in whatever I do. Let my work for You be done gladly. Amen.

HAPPY AT WORK

Color each chore item below. Draw a happy face on each one to help you remember to be glad when you serve the Lord at home.

STEPHEN

I love Jesus more than anything.
Love the Lord our God with all your heart.

Deuteronomy 6:5

Throwing Stones

Dad gave Ray a big hug as he tucked him into bed. "I love you, buddy," he said.

"How much do you love me, Dad?" asked Ray.

"I love you more than the whole world," said Dad.

"Would you do anything for me?" Ray asked.

"Yes!" replied Dad. "I would do anything for you."

"Would you eat bugs for me?" asked Ray.

"Yes, I would eat bugs for you."

"Would you eat frog lips for me?"

"Yes, I would eat frog lips for you. I would even die for you, Ray. A man in the Bible named Stephen did that. He died for Jesus."

"What happened to him?" asked Ray.

"Stephen was filled with God's love and power," answered Dad. "He did many miracles in Jesus' name. But church leaders got mad at Stephen. They began to tell lies about Stephen. They said he was against God.

"Stephen told them, 'You have the law God put in place. But, you don't obey it.' The leaders threw stones at him.

"As the stones hit him, Stephen prayed, 'Lord Jesus, take me to heaven. Don't blame them for this sin.' After he said that, he died."

"Wow," said Ray. "Stephen must have loved Jesus very much."

"Yes," said Dad. "That is the kind of love I have for you, Ray."

Your Turn

1. Why did the leaders kill Stephen?
2. How can you show Jesus you love Him?

Prayer

Dear Jesus, I love You. I love You more than any of my toys. I love You more than my bike. Show me how to love You more. Amen.

STONY PUZZLE

Match the words with the pictures on the stones. What is the message? The answer is on page 232.

STEPHEN

I can't see Jesus, but I love Him.
Blessed are those who have not seen and yet have believed.

John 20:29

Loving Jesus

Doug and his mother walked down the hall of St. James Hospital. Grandpa was in Room 342.

Doug stopped in the middle of the hall. "Look, Mom! Is this a real picture of Jesus? Is this what He really looked like?" asked Doug.

"I don't know, Doug. Nobody really knows what He looked like," said Mom. "There were no cameras that long ago."

"I'd like to see Jesus and know what He really looks like," said Doug.

"Would that make you love Him more, Doug?" asked Mom.

"No!" answered Doug. "I love Him even though I can't see Him. It doesn't matter to me what He looks like. I know what He has done for me. Besides, I belong to Him."

Mom put her hand on Doug's shoulder. "The Bible tells about a friend of Jesus' named Peter who said, 'You don't need to see Jesus to love Him.' And Jesus said in John 20:29, 'Blessed are those who have not seen and yet have believed.' Let's go see Grandpa now."

Your Turn

1. How can you love someone you can't see?
2. How can you show Jesus you love Him?

_____

_____

_____

_____

_____

_____

Prayer

I love You, Jesus, even though I can't see You. I don't need to see You to love You. I love You because You love me and died for me. Amen.

DRAWING JESUS

There were no cameras when Jesus walked the earth. Pretend you are able to take a picture of Jesus. Draw a picture of what you think Jesus looks like inside the frame below.

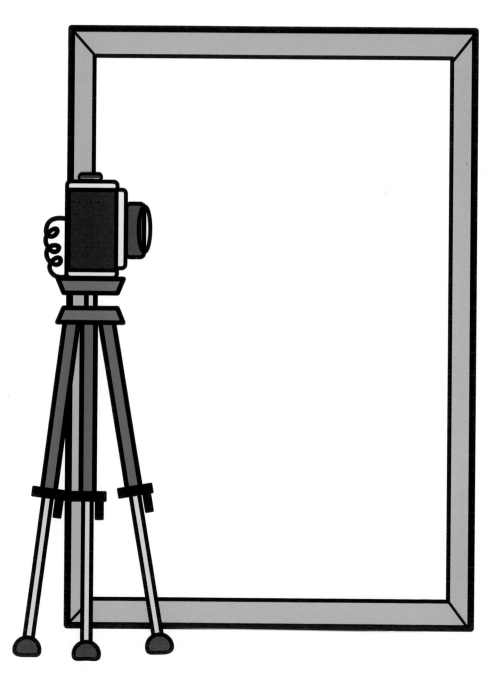

PAUL

Paul shared God's word.

Therefore go and make disciples of all nations, baptizing them in the name of the Father and of the Son and of the Holy Spirit.
Matthew 28:19

The Tent Maker

Have you ever slept in a tent? A man in the Bible, called Paul, slept in a tent. He also made tents. In Bible times, tents were hand sown with big needles. Heavy cloth was cut to make the tents.

Paul made tents for money. He liked making tents. But he liked telling others about Jesus best of all. He traveled to tell people about Him. Paul opened the Bible scrolls to teach true things about God and Jesus. Paul wanted everyone to have a chance to hear the Word of God.

At one town He met a man named Aquila (a-KEE-lah) and his wife, Priscilla. Aquila and Priscilla were also tent makers. Paul spent many hours making tents with them. The couple let Paul stay in their home because they loved hearing him teach about Jesus. Paul loved talking to his new friends. They were glad they could listen to Paul.

Aquila and Priscilla said, "We will help Paul share God's Word with people in many places." They said good-bye to their friends and got into a boat to go to a new place to share about Jesus.

On Paul's travels, he met many new people. Sometimes he faced harm and danger on his trips. Paul was nearly killed when the ship he was on crashed. People who didn't like his talking about Jesus put him in jail. Paul didn't care what happened to him. He knew God wanted him to share the good news of Jesus with everyone he could.

You don't need to travel far away to share about God like Paul did. You can tell your friends and neighbors next door!

Your Turn

1. Why do you think Aquila and Priscilla liked being around Paul?
2. What are some ways to share Jesus with people who don't know Him?

_____

_____

_____

Prayer

Dear God, help me to share the love of Jesus with someone. Amen.

TENT MAKING

Make the tent below by following the numbers. Draw a picture on the tent of someone who you plan to tell about Jesus. Pray for that person and tell him or her about Jesus. The answer is on page 232.

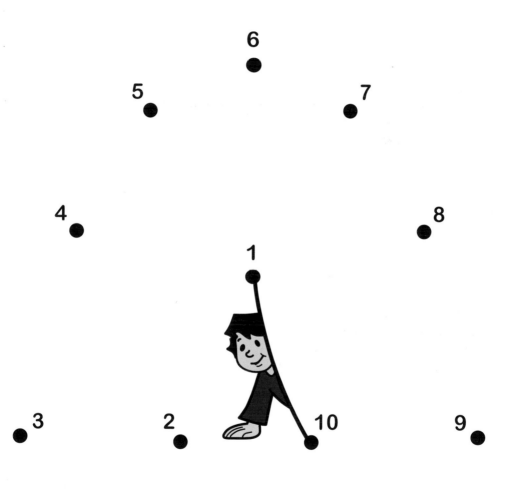

PAUL

I can share God's Word.
I am not ashamed [shy] *of the gospel,*
because it is the power of God.

Romans 1:16

The News

Ben handed the newspaper to his mom as he walked in the door from school.
"How was school today?" Mom asked.

"Great!" said Ben.

Mom opened the newspaper and read this story aloud to Ben:

Wil Conover testifies in trial

A 16-year-old boy told a jury how he saw a man running from First Bank the day of the robbery. The witness said he was leaving Fred's Grocery when he spotted the man running from the bank. Conover stated that the man was wearing a black mask and carrying a paper bag. Conover watched the man get into a car and drive away. The boy was able to remember the car's license plate numbers. The quick thinking boy allowed the police to catch the thief.

"I wonder if he was afraid?" asked Ben.

"I'm sure he was," said Mom. "But, his news needed to be reported."

Mom continued to study the paper as she talked. "Wil may have been afraid to tell what had happened. But reporting the truth was what God wanted him to do." God's words in the Bible also need to be reported. Don't be afraid to give that report from the Bible: God loved us so much that He sent His son to die for our sins. The Bible reports God's power to help us spread His love.

Your Turn

1. For what are God's words useful?
2. Do you know people who need to hear God's Word? Who are they?

Prayer

Dear God, help me to read Your word and tell others about the good news. Amen.

GOD'S HEADLINES

Make up your own newspaper headlines about Jesus. Think of something about Jesus that you need to report to a friend. Write it on the space below. You can draw a picture instead of writing a headline if you want.

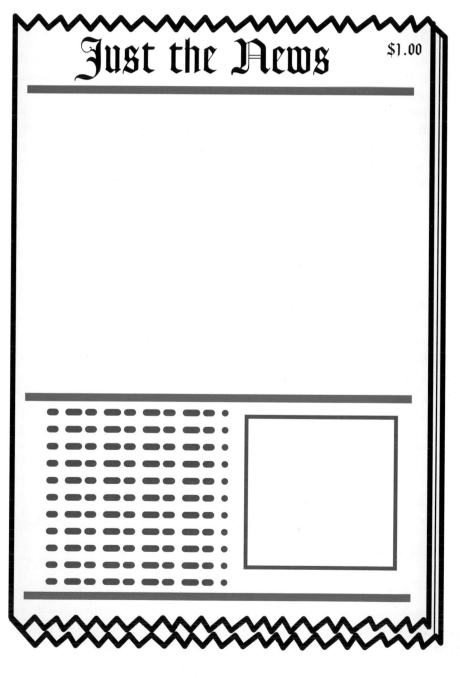

TIMOTHY

You can learn to count on God.
Timothy, my son whom I love, who is faithful in the Lord.
1 Corinthians 4:17

Timothy Was Counted On

Long ago there lived a boy named Timothy. Timothy lived with his mother, Eunice, and his grandmother, Lois. His mother and grandmother taught him how to love God.

Eunice and Lois read God's Word to Timothy and taught him about God. Timothy learned how to trust God to meet his needs. He sang praises to God each day.

Timothy also learned to pray. As Timothy grew, he learned to obey God. When his mother and grandmother needed help with chores, he could be counted on.

Soon Timothy grew into a man who loved God. One day, Paul, a man of God, came to town. He was looking for Timothy.

He said, "Timothy, I want you to come and help me tell people about Jesus." Paul had heard about Timothy and how he could be counted on. Paul wanted Timothy to travel to with him and share about God. Timothy worked hard for him. He was glad Paul asked him to share about Jesus. Paul counted on Timothy to be a faithful friend, too. Timothy was counted on by others.

Your Turn

1. How did Timothy learn to count on God?
2. What had Paul heard about Timothy?
3. What should you do to learn about God like Timothy did?

_____

_____

_____

_____

_____

Prayer

Dear God, thank You that my parents and Sunday school teachers are helping me learn about You. Make me someone whom others can count on. Amen.

TIMOTHY'S BACKPACK

Can you find the secret message in Timothy's backpack? Use the numbers on the backpack to read Timothy's message. Write each letter using the key from the road below. The answer is on page 232.

L	U	A	P	U	O	C	T	S	N	N	M	O	E
1	2	3	4	5	6	7	8	9	10	11	12	13	14

TIMOTHY

I can be counted on.
We know and rely on the love God has for us.

1 John 4:16

Count On Me

"Hello, Ken? This is Daniel. Want to come over?" Daniel asked Ken over the phone.

"We should practice the one-legged race for track day at school," said Daniel.

"Yeah!" said Ken.

Then Daniel asked, "Will you help me practice for the baseball toss too?"

"No problem!" replied Ken. "You can count on me."

Daniel had known Ken since they were babies. They had always been good friends. They counted on each other. Daniel was there when Ken fell out of the tree at the park and broke his leg. Daniel ran to a nearby house and got help for Ken. Ken was there when Daniel won the school spelling contest and received a prize. The boys knew they would always be there for each other when one of them needed help from the other. Each boy knew the other could be counted on. Can you be counted on?

Your Turn

1. Who counts on you?
2. How can you show friends you can be counted on?
3. How can you help others count on God?

_____

_____

_____

_____

_____

_____

Prayer

God, I want people to be able to count on me. Show me how I can be counted on by others. Amen.

BASEBALL TOSS

Draw a picture of a friend you count on next to Daniel as he tosses the ball.

ANSWER KEY

page 13

page 75

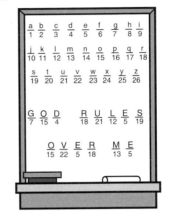

```
a  b  c  d  e  f  g  h  i
1  2  3  4  5  6  7  8  9

j  k  l  m  n  o  p  q  r
10 11 12 13 14 15 16 17 18

s  t  u  v  w  x  y  z
19 20 21 22 23 24 25 26


G  O  D        R  U  L  E  S
7  15 4        18 21 12 5  19


   O  V  E  R        M  E
   15 22 5  18       13 5
```

page 15

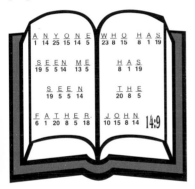

```
A  N  Y  O  N  E       W  H  O       H  A  S
1  14 25 15 14 5       23 8  15      8  1  19

   S  E  E  N     M  E          H  A  S
   19 5  5  14    13 5          8  1  19

       S  E  E  N           T  H  E
       19 5  5  14          20 8  5

F  A  T  H  E  R.     J  O  H  N
6  1  20 8  5  18     10 15 8  14    14:9
```

page 101

page 63

1. Balaam doesn't want to listen to God or obey God.

2. Balaam doesn't want to listen to God, but he will obey Him.

3. Balaam wants to listen to God and obey Him.

page 103

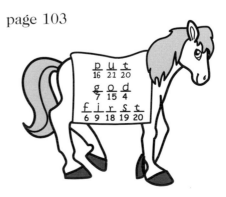

```
p  u  t
16 21 20
g  o  d
7  15 4
f  i  r  s  t
6  9  18 19 20
```

ANSWER KEY

page 121

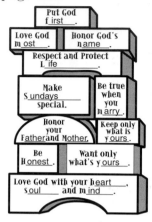

Put God f_irst_.

Love God m_ost_.

Honor God's n_ame_.

Respect and Protect L_ife_.

Make S_undays_ special.

Be true when you m_arry_.

Honor your Father_and_ Mother_._

Keep only what is y_ours_.

Be H_onest_.

Want only what's y_ours_.

Love God with your h_eart_, S_oul_ and m_ind_.

page 123

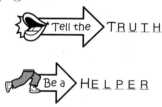

Tell the → TR_U_T_H_

Be a → H_E_L_P_E_R

Give a → H_U_G

page 131

I WILL NOT
1   2 3 4 5   6 7 8

FORGET YOU!
9 10 11 12 13 14   15 16 17

page 137

I AM WONDERFULLY
① ②③ ④⑤⑥⑦⑧⑨⑩⑪⑫⑬⑭

MADE
⑮⑯⑰⑱

page 143

Th_os_E wh_o_ b_E_li_e_v_e_
i_N_ H_i_s N_a_me,
He gave t_H_ _E_
r_i_ght t_o_
be_C_ o_M_e
chi_l_dre_N_
_o_f G_O_D.
John 1:12

page 149

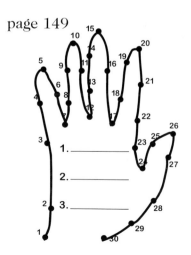

1. _____
2. _____
3. _____

230

ANSWER KEY

page 151

page 207

page 153

page 163

RETURN TO ME FOR
  1   2   3   4

YOU BELONG TO ME
 5   6   7   8

page 209

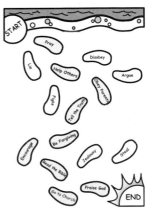

page 211

ANSWER KEY

page 217

page 221

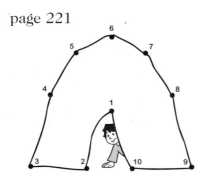

page 225